GW00382225

ECDL® 5.0

European Computer Driving Licence

Module 2 - IT User Fundamentals

using Windows XP with Office 2007

This training, which has been approved by ECDL Foundation, includes exercise items intended to assist Candidates in their training for an ECDL Certification Programme. These exercises are not ECDL Foundation certification tests. For information about authorised Test Centres in different national territories, please refer to the ECDL Foundation website at www.ecdl.org

Release BCS011v2

Published by:

CiA Training Ltd
Business & Innovation Centre
Sunderland Enterprise Park
Sunderland SR5 2TH
United Kingdom

Tel: +44 (0) 191 549 5002
Fax: +44 (0) 191 549 9005

E-mail: info@ciatraining.co.uk
Web: www.ciatraining.co.uk

ISBN 13: 978 1 86005 825 7

First published 2009

Copyright © 2009 CiA Training Ltd

Downloading the Data Files

The data associated with these exercises must be downloaded from our website. Go to: *www.ciatraining.co.uk/data*. Follow the on screen instructions to download the appropriate Office 2007 data files.

By default, the data files will be downloaded to **My Documents \ CIA DATA FILES \ ECDL \ 2 Managing Files**.

If you prefer, the data can be supplied on CD at an additional cost. Contact the Sales team at *info@ciatraining.co.uk*.

Aims

To familiarise the user with the main operating features of *Windows XP,* the **Desktop**, application windows and display settings. To demonstrate the ability to manage files and organise folders. Use a word processing application and understand the basic operations associated with creating and editing a word processed document. To understand the importance of maintenance of IT systems and how to tackle common problems. To be aware of security issues and laws and guidance covering the use of IT.

Objectives

After completing the guide the user will be able to:

- Use the main features of the operating system, including adjusting the main computer settings and using built-in help features

- Operate effectively around the computer desktop and work effectively in a graphical user environment

- Know about the main concepts of file management and be able to efficiently organise files and folders so that they are easy to identify and find

- Use utility software to compress and extract large files and use anti-virus software to protect against computer viruses

- Demonstrate the ability to use simple text editing and print tools available within the operating system

Assessment of Knowledge

At the end of this guide is a section called the **Record of Achievement Matrix**. Before the guide is started it is recommended that the user complete the matrix to measure the level of current knowledge.

Tick boxes are provided for each feature. **1** is for no knowledge, **2** some knowledge and **3** is for competent.

After working through a section, complete the **Record of Achievement** matrix for that section and only when competent in all areas move on to the next section.

Contents

Section 1
Getting Started

By the end of this Section you should be able to:

Appreciate Health & Safety and Legal Issues

Start, Restart and Close Down the Computer

Identify Parts of a Window

Understand Start Menu and Taskbar

Recognise and Arrange Desktop Icons

Open, Resize and Close Windows

View System Properties

Use Help

To gain an understanding of the above features, work through the **Driving Lessons** in this **Section**.

For each **Driving Lesson**, read the **Park and Read** instructions, without touching the keyboard, then work through the numbered steps of the **Manoeuvres** on the computer. Complete the **Revision Exercise(s)** at the end of the section to test your knowledge.

Driving Lesson 1 - Preparation

Park and Read

Health and Safety

Before you turn a computer on, you have to make sure you will be able to use it safely; this means safe for you as a user and safe for other people. Your work station must conform to the relevant Health and Safety at Work (HASAW) legislation. A workplace that has swivel chairs with adjustable positions, stable, roomy desks, etc., will provide a working environment that is comfortable and safe. Furniture and equipment should be suitably positioned and conform to any necessary regulations. It should be arranged to provide the user with a safe and comfortable environment. Injuries common in an IT environment are:

- Aches and pains due to bad posture when seated for long periods

- Repetitive strain injury (RSI) caused by poor position of the seat/desk combined with repeated movements of the same joints over a long period of time

- Paper cuts from refilling printers/photocopiers

- Eye strain which can be caused by glare or flickering from a VDU and by not taking regular visual breaks (10 minutes every hour is recommended) away from the screen

- Electric shocks due to incorrect working practice or dangerous wiring

- Injuries due to tripping over trailing wires or other obstructions.

　*See **Driving Lesson 68 Health and Safety** for further information.*

Laws and Guidelines

There are many rules and regulations that affect how you use IT on a daily basis. You need to be aware of these and consider how they affect you personally.

Data Protection

The Data Protection Act (1998) regulates the use of personal data by all businesses. Personal data is any data that can be used to identify a living individual; it includes names, addresses, personalised e-mail addresses and video images of such individuals.

Driving Lesson 1 - Continued

Copyright

The effect of copyright on the day to day use of IT is that any text or picture scanned into a PC and saved, any graphic image, text file, audio or video file downloaded from the Internet and saved to disk is illegal, unless specifically identified by its owner as being copyright-free. This also applies to any digital material saved to any storage device.

 See **Driving Lesson 72 Copyright** *for further information.*

Equal Opportunities

You must conform to equal opportunities guidelines by making sure that nothing you produce could be offensive to those viewing it on grounds of gender, ethnic origin, religion, sexual orientation or disability.

Disability

There are also laws to ensure that people with disabilities are able to use IT in the same way as those without disabilities. This may mean the provision of specially adapted hardware such as mice, or software such as screen readers, voice recognition or magnifiers. This can also affect what you produce, for example web pages - these must be accessible to people with disabilities and there are certain standards that should be followed. The World Wide Web Consortium (W3C) develops and maintains web standards, which include the WAI - Web Accessibility Initiative.

 Manoeuvres

1. Think about how the legal issues mentioned above apply to you at work.

2. Make sure your chair is at the correct height and angle so that you can sit comfortably at the computer. Your feet should be flat on the floor and your back should be straight.

3. Make sure that you can see the screen properly and that there is no glare. You can change the angle of the monitor if necessary.

4. When you are entirely comfortable, move on to the next exercise.

Driving Lesson 2 - Starting the Computer

▣ Park and Read

A computer consists of various parts: a processing unit, keyboard, monitor, mouse and, optionally, a printer. The processing unit is switched on to start the computer. When the computer has started up, you may be required to log on to identify yourself. For security reasons this is done using a user name and password.

☞ Manoeuvres

1. Before switching a computer on, check for lights, usually green, on the front of the computer which shows that it is already on.

CD-ROM Drive

Monitor

Floppy Disk Drive

Case contains Processing Unit

Keyboard

Mouse

Power Switch

USB ports may be found here

2. If there is a light on but the screen is blank, the computer is in a dormant state; either move the mouse or press a key on the keyboard, otherwise:

3. Check the floppy drive for disks. If there is a disk in the drive, remove it.

4. Press the **Power Switch** on the front of the computer (some computers may have the power switch at the back).

5. If the monitor power light does not come on, press the monitor power button (some monitors take their power from the computer, so that the computer powers the monitor).

Driving Lesson 2 - Continued

6.   When both units are powered the computer goes through a startup routine and displays information on the screen.

7.   After various checks the *Windows* operating system is loaded.

8.   *Windows XP* allows more than one user to sign on to the same computer and maintain their own profile. If there is more than one profile on the machine a screen will be displayed to allow the correct profile to be selected.

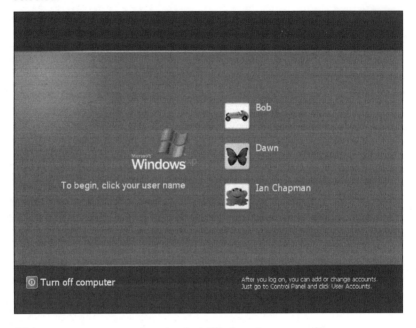

9.   Click your user name or icon to start *Windows* in your profile.

10.   If the computer you are working on is networked (joined to other computers), a **Log on to Windows** dialog box may appear, prompting for a password. Enter your **User name** and **Password**, then click on **OK**. Alternatively, depending on how the computer has been set up, *Windows* may start without the need to log on.

11.   The *Windows* **Desktop** screen is displayed.

Driving Lesson 3 - The Windows Desktop

▣ Park and Read

The **Desktop** may be customised according to the user's preference; every aspect of its appearance can be changed. For example, the general style of the screens can be set to **Classic** (to resemble previous Windows versions) or **XP** (as shown in this guide). For this reason, ***the screens shown in this guide may not quite match that of your computer***. The basic layout, however, should be the same.

☞ Manoeuvres

1.   The screen shows the **Desktop**. This is the starting point for all tasks performed in *Windows*. From here it is possible to access all the programs on the computer, perform file management tasks and use all the features of *Windows*.

2.   The screen is similar to that shown below; although the screen is shown after some icons have been added. The **Desktop** for a new system will have only a **Taskbar** and a **Recycle Bin**.

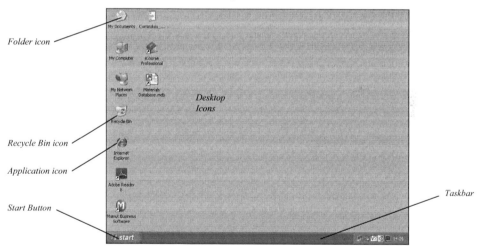

3.   The **Desktop** is divided into two parts. Along the bottom of the screen is a bar known as the **Taskbar**. This is used as a quick way to access certain features. This bar usually remains on screen at all times. The remainder of the **Desktop** is taken up by icons.

4.   These icons (small graphics with text underneath) represent programs saved on the **Desktop** or shortcuts that lead directly to a program, folder, file, etc. These icons will be used later. New icons will also be created.

Driving Lesson 4 - Arranging Icons

🅿 Park and Read

Icons on the **Desktop** can be arranged into any suitable order.

Nearly all *Windows* tasks can be performed using the mouse. There are a few different mouse techniques, they are:

Point	*position the mouse pointer until the tip of the pointer rests on the required position*
Click	*press and immediately release the left mouse button without moving the mouse*
Double click	*click the left mouse button twice in quick succession without moving the mouse*
Drag	*press the left mouse button and hold it down while the mouse is moved, then release the button at the appropriate location*

ℹ️ *Both the left and right mouse buttons are used to perform tasks in Windows, unless otherwise instructed, use the left mouse button.*

Icons in any window, or on the **Desktop**, can be clicked and dragged to any position required. They will then stay in position until moved again.

〽 Manoeuvres

1. Move the mouse around the desk. The mouse pointer will move around the screen, in the direction of the mouse movement.

2. Move the mouse pointer over one of the icons on the screen, such as the **Recycle Bin** icon. Click once and the icon and its associated label change appearance to show that it has been selected.

3. Move the mouse pointer to a clear part of the **Desktop** and click to deselect the icon.

4. Move the mouse pointer over a blank part of the **Desktop** and click once with the **right** mouse button. A **Shortcut Menu** is displayed.

Driving Lesson 4 - Continued

5. Without clicking, place the mouse pointer over **Arrange Icons By**. If **Auto Arrange** is ticked, then click on **Auto Arrange** to turn it off (**Auto Arrange** keeps the icons in place on the left, so they cannot be moved). If not, click anywhere on the **Desktop** away from the menus.

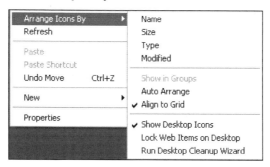

6. With **Auto Arrange** turned off the icons can be moved around. Click on any icon and hold the mouse button down. Drag the icon around the screen by moving the mouse, release the mouse button.

7. Move the icon back to its original position.

8. By clicking and dragging, move some of the icons around the **Desktop**.

9. Click with the **right** mouse button again, select **Arrange Icons By** option and then **Name**. The icons on the **Desktop** are now arranged neatly in order of name.

*If no new shortcut icons have been created on the **Desktop**, **Arrange Icons By** may have no effect as they may be already arranged by name.*

10. Click with the **right** mouse button again and select **Arrange Icons By | Size**. The icons are now arranged with the largest file first (this option works better when other shortcut icons have been added to the **Desktop**).

11. Rearrange the icons by **Name** again.

Driving Lesson 5 - The Taskbar

▣ Park and Read

The **Taskbar** is displayed across the bottom of the screen. The **Start** button is on the left. Some **Quick Launch** buttons may be displayed next to this on the right. The buttons seen on the **Taskbar** depend on which options have been selected.

More than one program may run at the same time (multi-tasking). As each program is started, a button appears on the **Taskbar**, with the program's name and a small icon.

The **Taskbar** button for the **active** program, i.e. the one that is currently being used, appears darker or **pressed**.

⌐ Manoeuvres

1. Place the mouse pointer over the **Start** button. A **ToolTip** is displayed, **Click here to begin**.

2. The centre part of the **Taskbar** is blank at the moment but is used to display program buttons (covered later).

ⅰ *There may be some other buttons on the **Taskbar** this is dependent upon which programs or shortcuts have been attached to it.*

3. The icons at the right of the **Taskbar** will include the **Date/Time** and may include **Volume** if it has been set up. These are covered later.

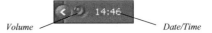
Volume   *Date/Time*

4. To move or resize the **Taskbar**, it must be unlocked. Right click on an unoccupied area on the **Taskbar** and click **Lock the Taskbar** to remove the check and unlock the bar.

5. Point to any unoccupied area on the **Taskbar**, then click and drag to the right of the screen. Move the **Taskbar** to the left of the screen and then drag it back to its original position at the bottom.

6. Move the mouse pointer slowly over the upper edge of the **Taskbar**. The mouse pointer will change shape into a double-headed arrow, ⬍. Click and drag this **Adjust** cursor up slightly to double the size of the **Taskbar** (useful if many programs are open).

7. Reduce the size of the **Taskbar** to its default size, i.e. one line.

8. Lock the **Taskbar** again by right clicking on it and selecting **Lock the Taskbar**.

Driving Lesson 6 - The Start Menu

▣ Park and Read

At the left of the **Taskbar**, at the bottom of the screen, is the **Start** button,

start. This button is used to start any program that is loaded on the computer and has been included in the menus.

⌐ Manoeuvres

1.   Click on the **Start** button to display the **Start** menu.

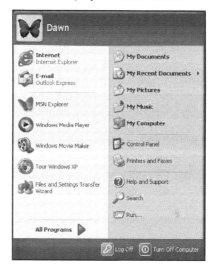

2.   The **Start** menu has two areas. At the left are the most recently used programs, which will vary as different programs are used, and at the right are the permanent **Start** options, which vary depending on how the computer has been set up. The main fixed **Start** menu options are:

All Programs	*gives quick access to all programs and accessories*
My Documents	*gives quick access to **My Documents** folder where letters and other personal documents may be stored*
My Recent Documents	*a list of the most recently opened documents*
My Pictures	*gives access to **My Pictures** – storage for all types of image file*

Driving Lesson 6 - Continued

My Music	*gives access to **My Music** – storage for all types of sound file*
My Computer	*gives access to information about drives and hardware on the computer*
My Network Places	*manages network and internet connections (when available)*
Control Panel	*allows control over the settings and options for all hardware and software on the computer*
Printers and Faxes	*change settings for existing devices or add new ones*
Help and Support	*gives access to the Windows **Help** system*
Search	*allows searching to find text, files, folders, etc.*
Run	*allows programs to be run or installed*
Log Off	*used for multiple users*
Turn Off Computer	*gives options to shut down or restart the computer.*

3. Leave the mouse pointer over **All Programs** for a second or two. A new menu will appear (it may be different to that shown below).

4. Move the mouse pointer over the **Accessories** group, to display that menu.

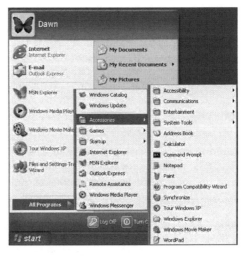

Driving Lesson 6 - Continued

5.   Move the mouse over the **System Tools** option, to view that menu.

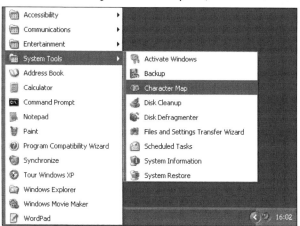

6.   The programs held in the **System Tools** menu are now listed. Press the **Escape <Esc>** key on the keyboard to remove the menu. Keep pressing **<Esc>** until no menus are displayed.

7.   Click **Start** and place the pointer over **My Recent Documents**. A list of the 15 files (of any type) last used by the system is displayed. The contents will be different on any system and for a new system the list may be empty.

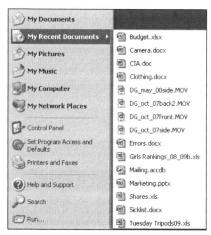

[i]   *Applications may be started from this list. Clicking on* **Camera.docx**, *in the example above, would start* **Word** *with* **Camera** *as the open document.*

8.   Click once on any blank part of the **Desktop**. This is an easier method of cancelling any menus.

Driving Lesson 7 - Opening Windows

🅿 Park and Read

Windows are rectangular areas of the screen in which programs are run, or system data is presented. All windows have similar properties although there are differences between the two types mentioned above. Many windows can be open at a time, each performing a different task.

Manoeuvres

1. Select **Start | My Computer**.

2. The **My Computer** window will open (there are many ways of displaying this screen so it may look different to that shown below).

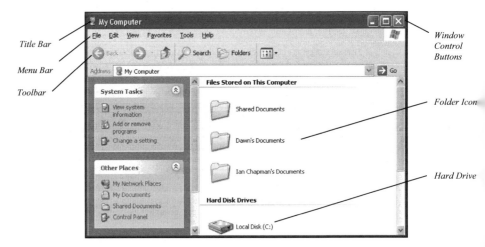

ℹ️ *If the window fills the screen, click the centre one of the* ***Window Control Buttons*** *at the top right, the* ***Restore Down*** *button* 🗗 *to reduce the size of the window.*

3. A named button, , is displayed on the **Taskbar**. Each opened window is represented by a button on the **Taskbar**.

4. Each window is similar in its construction. A **Title Bar** is across the top, coloured blue by default. On the **Title Bar** are three **Window Control Buttons** at the top right. These are **Minimize**, 🗕, **Maximize**, 🗖, and **Close**, ✖, buttons.

Driving Lesson 7 - Continued

5. The **Maximize** button increases the size of the window to its maximum size, probably filling the screen. Click the **Maximize** button of the **My Computer** window.

6. When a window is maximised, the **Maximize** button is replaced by the **Restore Down** button, 🗗. Click the **Restore Down** button to change the maximised window back to its previous size.

7. The **Minimize** button 🗖 hides the window completely. Click the **Minimize** button 🗖 of the **My Computer** window.

8. However, the program or task in the window is not ended and the window can be re-activated by clicking on the named button on the **Taskbar**, at the bottom of the screen. Click the **My Computer** icon on the **Taskbar** to redisplay the window, then use the **Maximize** button to expand it.

9. Below the **Title Bar** is the **Menu Bar**. Click on a menu and view the attached list. Note that some of the items may be ghosted, greyed out, this means that they are not available under the present circumstances. Move the mouse pointer along the **Menu Bar** to display the other lists.

10. Click on the selected menu again or click on any blank part of the window to remove the menu.

11. Below the **Menu Bar** is the **Toolbar**. This is a row of buttons to quickly achieve tasks without using the menu alternative. Some buttons may not have names. Move the mouse over one of these and leave it there for a few seconds. A **ToolTip** will appear, giving the button name.

12. The main part of the window is split between information on the left and the icons on the right. Click on the **Hard Drive** icon 🖴 Local Disk (C:), it changes to 🖴 Local Disk (C:) when selected (the hand on the icon indicates a shared drive and may not be present). The amount of used and free space is displayed under **Details** on the left.

13. Click once on each icon, and read the associated information.

14. Click on the hard drive **Local Disk C:** and select **File | Properties** from the **Menu Bar** to display more detailed properties information. Click the **OK** button to close the **Properties** dialog box.

15. Restore the **My Computer** window to its previous size.

16. The window may have a **Scroll Bar** displayed. This is covered in a later Driving Lesson.

Driving Lesson 8 - Sizing and Moving Windows

◘ Park and Read

If a window is not maximised (filling the whole screen), the size and position of it can be changed.

↱ Manoeuvres

1.   Move the mouse pointer over the **Title Bar** of the **My Computer** window.

2.   Click and drag downwards. The entire window will move down, be careful not to move any part of the window off the screen. Release the mouse button.

3.   The size of the window can be changed. Move the mouse pointer over the right edge of the window, until the pointer changes to a black double headed arrow, .

4.   Click and drag to the right, and then release the mouse button, to increase the width of the window.

5.   Placing the mouse over a corner of a window allows a two directional change in the size of a window. Place the mouse pointer over the bottom right corner of the **My Computer** window.

6.   The cursor changes to two headed diagonal arrow, . Click and drag a small amount in any direction to change the size and scale of the window.

Driving Lesson 9 - Scroll Bars

🅿 Park and Read

When a **Window** in any application is too small to display all the information in it, the window automatically adds **scroll bars**. Scroll bars are added horizontally and/or vertically, depending on the hidden information. Scroll bars are used in many other places where there is hidden data, for example in drop down lists.

👉 Manoeuvres

1.   The **My Computer** window should still be open. If not, double click on the **My Computer** icon to open it. If there is no icon on the **Desktop**, click **Start** and right click on **My Computer**, then click **Show on Desktop**.

2.   Click the **Control Panel** link in **Other Places** at the left of the **My Computer** window. The **Control Panel** dialog box is opened. Note the **Control Panel** button on the **Taskbar**.

3.   There are many more icons inside this window. The contents of this window are covered in a later section. If the window fills the screen, click the **Restore Down** button, 🗗, to place the **Control Panel** in its own window.

4.   Reduce the size of the window so that the vertical **Scroll Bar** is displayed.

5.   If the window does not look like the diagram below, click **Switch to Classic View** at the left of the screen.

Vertical Scroll Bar

Driving Lesson 9 - Continued

6.   The vertical scroll bar can be used to scroll up and down in the window. A scroll bar consists of scroll arrows at either end of the bar and a scroll button that shows the relative position of the current view. The scroll button can be moved by means of the arrows or by dragging.

7.   Click on the down arrow of the right vertical scroll bar to move the area displayed in the window down gradually. Continue to do this until the scroll button is at the bottom of the scroll bar.

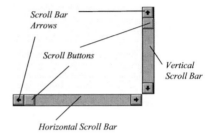

i *The scroll buttons reduce in size as the window becomes smaller, i.e. more information to scroll.*

8.   Click and drag the vertical scroll button to the top of the bar.

i *To move the display of a window up/down more quickly, click once on the vertical scroll bar between the scroll button and the top/bottom arrow.*

9.   Click **Switch to Category View** at the left of the window. This is the default view in *Windows XP*.

10. Leave the **Control Panel** window open.

Driving Lesson 10 - Close a Window

Park and Read

The **Close** button, ⊠, at the top right of every window, closes it and any task being performed within it. If there is a process running in a window, there may be a warning message before closing.

Manoeuvres

1. Click the **Close** button, ⊠, of the **Control Panel** window.

Close Button

2. The window is closed and **Control Panel** icon is removed from the **Taskbar**.

3. Double click on the **My Computer** icon on the **Desktop** to reopen it. If there is no icon on the **Desktop**, click **Start** and right click on **My Computer**, then click **Show on Desktop**.

4. An alternative method of closing a window is to click on the small icon to the left of the window name in the **Title Bar**. Click the icon, ▮, to display a window control menu.

5. The last item on the menu is **Close**. Select **Close**.

> *The window can also be closed by right clicking its icon on the **Taskbar** and selecting **Close** or by pressing <Alt F4>.*

⤢	Restore	
	Move	
	Size	
▬	Minimize	
☐	Maximize	
✕	Close	Alt+F4

Driving Lesson 11 - System Properties

▣ Park and Read

The **System Properties** can be viewed to show information relating to the computer.

☞ Manoeuvres

1. Right click on the **My Computer** icon from the **Start** menu or from the **Desktop**.

2. Select **Properties** from the shortcut menu.

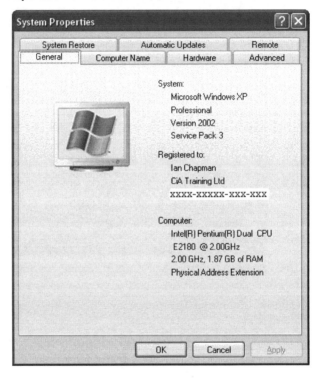

3. With the **General** tab selected, read the information. The operating system and version number are shown under **System** and the type of chip, the processor and the amount of memory are displayed under **Computer**.

4. Click the **Computer Name** tab to display information on the computer name and workgroup.

Driving Lesson 11 - Continued

5.   Click the **Hardware** tab then the **Device Manager** button to display information on the different parts of the computer.

i   *An error message may be displayed if you do not have the required security privileges to change any settings. Click* **OK** *to continue.*

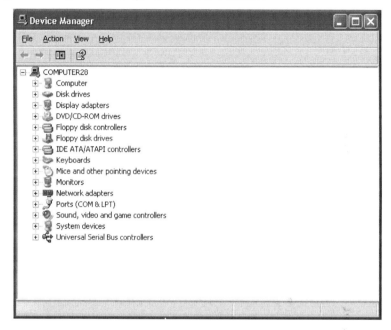

6.   A list of all attached device types will appear (it may be different to that above).

7.   Click on the ⊞ symbol next to a device type. The exact make and model of any device(s) of this type which are present will be listed. To see more information on any device, right click on the device name and then select **Properties** from the shortcut menu.

8.   Do not change any of the properties. Click the **Close** button twice to return to the **System Properties** dialog box.

9.   Click on the **Advanced** tab. Changes can be made with regard to **Performance, User Profiles** and **Startup and Recovery** settings.

10. Click the **Settings** button under each heading to view the settings, clicking **Cancel** in each new dialog box to return to **System Properties**.

11. Click the **Cancel** button to close the **System Properties** dialog box and return to the **Desktop**.

Driving Lesson 12 - Using Help

🅿 Park and Read

Windows has a built in **Help** facility to assist the user when information is required.

☞ Manoeuvres

1. Select the **Start** button and then select **Help and Support**.

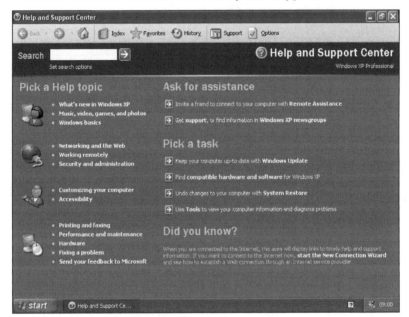

2. Move the mouse over each of the buttons on the toolbar to display a **ToolTip** about the button's function.

3. Click the **Index** button ⬚ Index on the toolbar.

4. **Index** gives an alphabetic list of every available help topic and can be searched using the scroll bar. The required topic can also be quickly found by entering it in the box above the list. Using the scroll bar, move down the list until **adjusting volume** is visible. Click on this topic, then click on **Display** to see the help on the right.

5. To obtain a printed copy of this information, click the **Print** button,

Driving Lesson 12 - Continued

6. With the **Index** still open, click in the **Type in the keyword to find** box, delete the contents and enter the word **background**.

7. In the topic list below, under the topic **backgrounds and themes** click on **changing**.

8. Click the **Display** button and in the **Topics Found** dialog box select **To change your desktop background** and click **Display**. **Help** is displayed on the right.

9. Click the **Home** button , , to return to the **Help and Support Center** window.

10. The **Search** box just under the toolbar can also be used to find help.

11. Type **printer drivers** in the **Search** box and click **Start searching**, .

12. From **Search Results**, click on **Printer drivers overview** and read the help at the right.

13. Click the **Home** button again to return to the **Help and Support Center** window.

14. Help can be accessed in a more general way by using the **Topics**. Click **What's new in Windows XP**.

15. Click at the left of **Windows Components**. Click **Accessories** and from the right of the window click **Using Paint**.

16. Read the help text then close the **Help and Support Center** window by clicking its **Close** button, .

Driving Lesson 13 - Shut Down and Restart

▣ Park and Read

If a computer is shut down abnormally, i.e. switched off in mid task, any unsaved data in an application can be lost and storage space within the computer can be corrupted. Shutting down properly prevents this and ensures that programs are closed and all data is saved correctly.

Normally, you should never need to reset the computer, while switched on. Sometimes, however, there may be problems and the computer could lock up, which means that it does not respond to moving the mouse or any key presses. The only course of action in this circumstance is to reset the computer.

⌒ Manoeuvres

1.   To close *Windows*, make sure all applications are closed, select **Start** and then click ⏻ Turn Off Computer. The **Turn off** options are displayed (**Hibernate** may be replaced by **Stand by** on some installations).

2.   If you wish to turn off the computer now click **Turn Off**.

> ℹ️ *If you do not want to shut down now, click **Cancel** to return to the **Desktop**.*

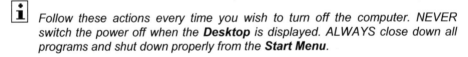

3.   Systems will be shut down correctly and when the message appears informing you to switch off, do so. Note some computers switch themselves off. If the monitor light remains on, switch the monitor off as well. The computer is now switched off completely.

> ℹ️ *Follow these actions every time you wish to turn off the computer. NEVER switch the power off when the **Desktop** is displayed. ALWAYS close down all programs and shut down properly from the **Start Menu**.*

4.   Turn the computer on and wait until *Windows* is running normally.

5.   The computer can be restarted using several methods: a) select **Restart** from the **Turn off** options, b) via a **Reset** button and c) using a key press <**Ctrl**> <**Alt**> <**Delete**> twice (<**Ctrl**> and <**Alt**> must be held down until <**Delete**> is pressed and then released). Use the first method, click **Start**, then **Turn Off Computer** then select the **Restart** option. Click **OK**.

> ℹ️ *The **Reset** button on the front of most computers must be used to restart if the keyboard and the mouse are not responding. If an application becomes unresponsive, press <**Ctrl Alt Delete**> to display the **Task Manager**. Select the application from the list and click **End Now**.*

Driving Lesson 14 - Revision

This Driving Lesson covers the features introduced in this section. Try not to refer to the previous Driving Lessons while completing it.

1. Begin this Driving Lesson with the computer switched off. Start the computer.

2. Move the **My Computer** icon to the top right of the screen.

3. **Auto Arrange** the **Desktop** icons.

4. Arrange the **Desktop** icons **by Type**.

5. Turn off **Auto Arrange**.

6. Display the **Control Panel** window.

7. Reduce the size of the window and move it to the top right corner of the screen.

8. **Maximise** the window, then **Restore** it.

9. Close the window.

10. Use the **Help Index** to find out about **Starting Programs | using Run command**. Read the **Help** window.

11. Close the **Help** window.

12. Close down the computer.

If you experienced any difficulty completing this Revision, refer back to the Driving Lessons in this section. Then redo the Revision.

Once you are confident with the features, complete the Record of Achievement Matrix referring to the section, at the end of the guide. Only when competent move on to the next Section.

Section 2
Managing Files

By the end of this Section you should be able to:

Understand Drives, Files and Folders

Understand File Types

Backup to a Removable Storage Device

Copy, Move, Rename and Delete Files/Folders

Create Folders

Use the Recycle Bin

Search for Files/Folders

To gain an understanding of the above features, work through the **Driving Lessons** in this **Section**.

For each **Driving Lesson**, read the **Park and Read** instructions, without touching the keyboard, then work through the numbered steps of the **Manoeuvres** on the computer. Complete the **Revision Exercise(s)** at the end of the section to test your knowledge.

Driving Lesson 15 - File Storage

▣ Park and Read

Computer systems store their data and programs on a variety of **Storage Devices**. The type and number of these devices can vary from one computer to another, but the operating system will always display the contents of these devices in a number of useful ways.

The vast majority of computers have a **Hard Disk Drive** (HDD) which is the main storage device for the system. These can store many Gigabytes of data, which can be accessed very quickly (access times measured in milliseconds). Traditionally this is referred to as drive **C**. It is possible however to have further such drives installed, which would then become drive **D**, etc.

Hard Disk Drives that are part of the computer are known as **Local Drives**, but if the computer is part of a network it may be possible to access the drives of other connected computers. These drives are then known as **Network Drives**.

Computers usually have a few **USB** drives. These are used to connect various devices to the computer. USB **flash memory** sticks can be attached in this way and used as a form of storage.

Often, when computers are networked, there will be an area for data storage on another machine, i.e. you may save your data to a drive on a remote computer, rather than to a drive on your own computer. This is called a **network drive**.

Online file storage is a facility that is becoming more popular. It allows you to save files to a specific hard drive on the Internet. There are many web sites that provide free online storage. With this convenient service, you can access your own files and share files via any PC with Internet access.

In a similar manner a **Compact Disk Drive** uses compact disks as the storage media, each compact disk holding at present about 700 Mb. Some drives will only read from existing CDs, others (CD writers) allow data to be written onto a blank CD; this is a CD-RW drive (Read Write). Most computers now have a DVD or DVD-RW drive; they are almost identical in principle to CD drives, but can hold several Gigabytes of data. CD/DVD devices are assigned drive letters after the last hard disk drive.

⌐ Manoeuvres

1. Start up the computer and open the **My Computer** window to display the storage devices available on your computer.

Driving Lesson 15 - Continued

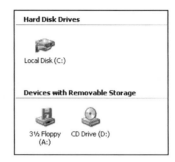

2. If the display is not in this form, select **View | Icons**. All icons may be shown together rather than grouped, but the icons themselves will be the same.

3. This is the display for a typical system and may be different on other computers. The hand symbol in the **Local Disk** icon indicates that the device may be shared by other computers on the network. This may not apply on your system.

4. The contents of any device can be displayed by double clicking the icon. Double click **Local Disk (C:)** to see the contents of the hard disk.

5. Close any open windows.

Driving Lesson 16 - Folders and Files

▶ Park and Read

In order to assist in storing and finding files and programs on the hard disk, *Windows* uses **Folders**. Any storage device, hard disk, floppy disk, memory stick or CD/DVD, can be split into many folders, each containing all the files related to a specific task or program. A folder may also contain other folders, thus sub-dividing the disk even further. The concept is much like organising a filing cabinet by having separate drawers and files for each particular task.

A folder in *Windows XP* appears as an icon, 📁, with the name of the folder printed next to or underneath it, depending on the view displayed. When the icon is double clicked, the folder opens, and its contents appear in a new window.

↱ Manoeuvres

1. Select **Start** then **My Documents** to open that folder and display its contents.

2. If the data files which accompany this guide have been installed correctly there will be a folder **CIA DATA FILES** within the **My Documents** folder. Double click that folder icon to display its contents. There will be a folder **ECDL** in the contents. Double click **ECDL** to display its contents (the appearance of this display may be different).

2 Managing Files   3 Word Processing   4 Spreadsheets   5 Databases   6 Presentations

3. Double click **2 Managing Files** to open the folder and display the files contained in it. Select **View | Details** to see the files listed in a more condensed view with more information.

4. If the file extensions are not displayed, select **Tools | Folder Options** and click on the **View** tab. Make sure that the **Hide extensions for known file types** is <u>unchecked</u>. Click **OK** to display the file extensions.

ℹ️ *Files are identified by extensions, e.g. .docx for a Word document, after the file name.*

5. There are 17 files displayed. These represent 10 different types of files. The **.avi** is a video file, **.wav** are sound files, the **.tif** and **.jpg** are image files, the **.docx** files are *Word* documents, **.txt** is a basic text file, the **.xlsx** is an *Excel* workbook, the **.accdb** is an *Access* database, the **.pptx** is a *PowerPoint* presentation and **.zip** is a compressed archive. File types are covered in more detail in a later Driving Lesson.

6. Close the open window using the **Close** button, ⊠.

Driving Lesson 17 - Folder View

▣ Park and Read

Folder View displays the organisation of files and folders in any open window. It organises the storage of data on a computer in a hierarchical way; that is, it will show the main devices available to the computer, each device can then be expanded to show the component folders and files, and each folder can be further expanded down to the lowest possible level. This view also shows the size of files and folders (see graphic on next page). They are measured in **KB**, **MB** and **GB**; the size of a spreadsheet file may be 50KB, a high quality image file perhaps 600KB, a folder containing many of these images possibly several MB. A folder containing your entire collection of digital photos may be several GB in size.

It can also be used to control the copying, moving, creating and deleting of files and folders, known as **File Management**. In previous versions of *Windows* this function was carried out using *Windows Explorer*. This program is still available and can be found under **Accessories**.

☞ Manoeuvres

1. Select **Start** then **My Computer** to open that window. Maximise the window if necessary.

2. Click on the **Folders** button, [Folders], on the toolbar to display the **Folders** window. Click on **Local Disk (C:)** on the left to display the folder structure in the **View** pane on the right.

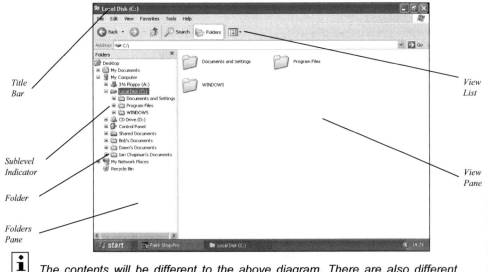

Title Bar

Sublevel Indicator

Folder

Folders Pane

View List

View Pane

ℹ️ *The contents will be different to the above diagram. There are also different views of the same information. The window above shows **View | Tiles**.*

Driving Lesson 17 - Continued

3.   On the left is the **Folders** pane, which shows the drives and folders on the computer. On the right is the **View** pane, showing the contents of the selected drive or folder.

4.   Click on any folder icon in the **Folders** pane. The contents of the folder are shown in the **View** pane.

5.   Select **View | Icons**. The folder contents are now shown as small icons.

6.   Select **View | Details**. The folder contents now have their name, size, type and date modified shown. This enables the smallest, largest, newest, oldest and files of the same type to be identified.

7.   In the **Folders** pane, scroll to **My Documents**, (there may be more than one **My Documents** folder, use the one highest in the **Folders** list, just under the **Desktop** entry). The folder has a ⊞ icon denoting that it has subfolders. Click once on it, the subfolders are displayed underneath the folder and it changes to a ⊟ icon. This is called *expanding* a folder.

8.   Expand the **CIA DATA FILES** folder.

9.   Expand the **ECDL** folder, this contains all the data files required to study for this qualification.

10. To hide the subfolders, click on the ⊟ icon next to expanded folders. A ⊟ icon changes to a ⊞ icon again and the subfolders or files are hidden. This is called *collapsing* a folder.

Views of drives can also be expanded and collapsed.

11. Expand the **ECDL** folder and then click once on the **2 Managing Files** folder to display the files in it. Make sure **Details** view is active.

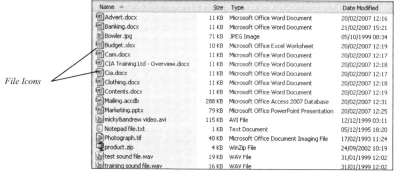

File Icons

12. Different types of files are displayed with a different icon before the name and the size, type and date when saved (modified) are all displayed.

13. There are no further folders within this display so no more expansion is possible. Leave the display open for the next exercise.

Driving Lesson 18 - File Types

▣ Park and Read

File types are represented by a 3 - 5 character file extension after a file name and tell the computer system what type of file it is. When a file is created by an application, e.g. spreadsheet, the correct file extension is automatically added. You can identify what type of file it is by the extension and the icon before the file name.

Care should be taken when copying or renaming files to maintain the correct file extension. Changing the file extension does not change the file contents but will confuse the computer operating system. For example, if a spreadsheet file is given a **.docx** extension and then double clicked, *Word* will attempt to open it and there will be an error.

Some common file types are listed here:

.docx	*Word 2007* document.
.accdb	*Access 2007* database.
.pptx	*PowerPoint 2007* presentation.
.xlsx	*Excel 2007* spreadsheet.
.avi, **.mpeg**	Video files.
.exe	Executable file, i.e. a program.
.jpg, **.tif**, **.gif**	Image files.
.tmp	Temporary file. One used by the system during a process and then deleted automatically.
.txt, **.rtf**	Generic text files.
.pdf	Portable document format files.
.wav, **.mp3**	Audio or Sound files.
.zip	A compressed (zipped) archive file. These are described in a later Section.

⌒ Manoeuvres

1. From the display of files in the **2 Managing Files** folder, identify each of the file types in the folder just by the icon and the file extension.

2. Display the contents of each of the other subfolders of **ECDL** in turn and identify all of the file types found there.

Driving Lesson 19 - Sorting File Displays

▣ Park and Read

The list of files shown in the **View Pane** of the **My Computer** display can be presented in different ways. As well as the different **View** options covered already, the files can be shown in different orders, i.e. sorted.

⌐ Manoeuvres

1. Use the **Folders Pane** to display a list of the files in the **2 Managing Files** folder. Adjust the column widths if necessary to display all data as below, To adjust the columns, click and drag the borders between columns on the **Header Bar**.

Name ▲	Size	Type	Date Modified
Advert.docx	11 KB	Microsoft Office Word Document	20/02/2007 12:16
Banking.docx	11 KB	Microsoft Office Word Document	21/02/2007 15:21
Bowler.jpg	71 KB	JPEG Image	05/10/1999 08:34
Budget.xlsx	10 KB	Microsoft Office Excel Worksheet	20/02/2007 12:19
Cam.docx	11 KB	Microsoft Office Word Document	20/02/2007 12:17
CIA Training Ltd - Overview.docx	11 KB	Microsoft Office Word Document	20/02/2007 12:18
Cia.docx	11 KB	Microsoft Office Word Document	20/02/2007 12:17
Clothing.docx	11 KB	Microsoft Office Word Document	20/02/2007 12:18
Contents.docx	11 KB	Microsoft Office Word Document	20/02/2007 12:19
Mailing.accdb	288 KB	Microsoft Office Access 2007 Database	20/02/2007 12:31
Marketing.pptx	79 KB	Microsoft Office PowerPoint Presentation	20/02/2007 12:25
micky&andrew video.avi	115 KB	AVI File	12/12/1999 03:11
Notepad file.txt	1 KB	Text Document	05/12/1995 18:20
Photograph.tif	48 KB	Microsoft Office Document Imaging File	17/02/1993 11:24
product.zip	4 KB	WinZip File	24/09/2002 10:19
test sound file.wav	19 KB	WAV File	31/01/1999 12:02
training sound file.wav	16 KB	WAV File	31/01/1999 12:02

Header Bar

2. The default sequence for the display is alphabetical by name. This is useful if you need to find a specifically named file. Click the **Name** column heading [Name ▲] to change the display to reverse alphabetic order.

3. Click the **Size** column heading to change the display order to ascending by size. Click it again to display in reverse order (descending), largest first. This is useful to find the largest files in a folder.

4. Click the **Type** column heading to sort the display by **File Type**. This will group all similar files and is useful if you want to see and count all the files of one type, e.g. all the *Word* documents.

5. The **Date Modified** column heading can be used to change the display order to the date the file was last accessed. This is useful to order the files in a folder so show those most recently used at the top.

6. Close the **My Computer** window.

Driving Lesson 20 - Creating New Folders

▣ Park and Read

New folders are created to organise files and keep files relating to a similar subject together. The **File | New | Folder** command can be used to create a new folder. Alternatively right clicking in the **View** pane of a folder and selecting **New | Folder** will create a new folder there. A folder within another folder is called a **subfolder**. When creating new folders (and files), take care to use meaningful names, so you will easily be able to organise and identify them later.

⌒ Manoeuvres

1. Open the **My Documents** window.

2. In **Folders view**, expand **CIA DATA FILES** then **ECDL**. Click on the **2 Managing Files** folder to display its contents.

3. To create a subfolder, select **File | New | Folder**. A new folder will appear with its name highlighted in blue, ready for the new name to be entered,

4. Type in the name **Reports**.

5. Press <**Enter**> to complete the process. The folder is now created and named. Notice the ⊞ sign next to **2 Managing Files** in the **Folders** window.

6. Right click in a blank area of the **View** pane of **2 Managing Files**. From the shortcut menu select **New** then **Folder** and name the new folder **Media**, press <**Enter**>. These folders within other folders are called **subfolders**.

7. Now select the **My Documents** folder in the **Folders** pane.

8. Select **File | New | Folder** from the menu. A new folder is created. Enter your own first name as the folder name and press <**Enter**>.

9. Select this new folder, create a subfolder within it and call the subfolder **Sample**. Your folder now has a ⊞ next to it.

10. Click on this to see the **Sample** subfolder within your own folder.

11. Open the **Sample** folder, it is empty.

12. Click the **Up** button, ▨ until you can view the contents of the **Desktop**.

Driving Lesson 21 - Copying Files and Folders

▣ Park and Read

To work with a file, click on it once, this highlights the file showing that it is selected.

Selected files can be copied in a variety of ways: by dragging from one location to another using the left or right mouse button or by using toolbar buttons.

Copying important files from the hard disk to a different drive, usually a CD or DVD, is known as creating a **backup**. These backup copies are an insurance against the original data ever being lost or corrupted, due to virus action, accidental deletion or catastrophic hard disk failure, for example. Backups should be made regularly and stored off site.

☞ Manoeuvres

1. Make sure a blank floppy disk is in the disk drive or an external storage device is attached to receive the copies.

2. In the **Folders** pane of the **Desktop**, expand the **My Documents** folder, (if the **Folders** pane is not displayed, click the [Folders] button). Expand the **CIA DATA FILES** folder then **ECDL**. Click on the **2 Managing Files** folder to display its contents in the **View** pane.

3. Expand **My Computer**, click and drag the file **Advert** across to the floppy disk [3½ Floppy (A:)] icon or other storage device in the **Folders** pane. Notice that the mouse pointer has a plus sign next to it, meaning that the file is being *copied*.

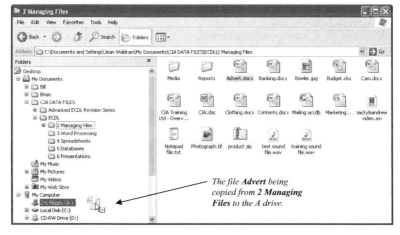

The file **Advert** being copied from **2 Managing Files** to the A drive.

Driving Lesson 21 - Continued

4. Release the mouse button. Because the file was dragged from one drive to another, **Copy** is the default action. An animation may be displayed.

When dragging within the same drive, hold down <Ctrl> to ensure a copy.

5. Repeat this process and drag across the **Banking** file to the same storage device.

6. Click on the storage device icon to check that there are two files present.

7. An alternative method of copying is to use the **Copy To Folder** command. Select the **2 Managing Files** folder and click once on the icon to select **Notepad file**.

8. Select **Edit | Copy To Folder**. A **Copy Items** dialog box is displayed.

9. Select the storage device, expanding **My Computer**, if necessary (**Floppy** drive shown in the diagram).

10. Click **Copy** to copy the file, then view the contents of the floppy disk to check that there are three files present.

The copying of important files from the hard drive to an external storage device is known as creating a Backup. The copy can be made by any method including dragging and the key presses <Ctrl C> for Copy and <Ctrl V> for Paste.

11. View the contents of **2 Managing Files**. Another way to copy files is to use the right mouse button. Using the right mouse button click and drag the **Cam** icon to the external storage device. Release the mouse button.

12. Select **Copy Here** from the shortcut menu to copy the file.

*The menu commands, **Edit | Copy** and **Edit | Paste**, can also be used to copy files or folders.*

13. Copying within the same folder produces a duplicate copy of a file. View the contents of the folder **2 Managing Files**. Click on the **Notepad file**, then use copy & paste to create **Copy of Notepad file** in the same folder.

14. Folders are copied in the same way as files. Select the **Sample** subfolder within your own folder and use any method already shown to copy the folder to **My Documents**.

Driving Lesson 22 - Moving Files and Folders

▣ Park and Read

Moving files and folders is similar to copying files and folders. A file or folder can be moved from one location to another on the same drive by dragging and dropping using the left mouse button (hold down **Shift** if moving to a different drive). Alternatively the **Move To** or **Cut and Paste** commands could be used to move files or folders to any location.

ⓘ *Clicking and dragging a file icon with the **right** mouse button will produce a shortcut menu when the button is released, select **Move Here**.*

⌁ Manoeuvres

1. Display the files within the **2 Managing Files** folder.

2. Make sure that the **2 Managing Files** folder is expanded to display the **Reports** and **Media** subfolders in the **Folders** pane.

3. Click and drag the file icon **Advert** from the **View** pane, to the **Reports** folder in the **Folders** pane, releasing the mouse button when over the folder. Notice that there is no ⊞ icon, indicating that the file is going to be *moved*. The file icon will disappear from the **2 Managing Files** pane.

4. Display the **Reports** folder. The **Advert** icon is displayed.

5. Select the **Cam** icon from the **2 Managing Files** folder and select **Edit | Move To Folder**.

6. The **Move Items** dialog box is displayed. Expand the **My Documents**, **CIA DATA FILES**, **ECDL** and **2 Managing Files** folders and then click on the **Reports** folder.

7. Click **Move** to move **Cam** to the **Reports** folder.

8. Drag to move the **CIA Training Ltd - Overview** and **Cia** files from the **2 Managing Files** folder to the **Reports** folder.

9. Select **Copy of Notepad file** from the **2 Managing Files** folder then hold down the right mouse button and drag to the external storage device.

10. Release the mouse and select **Move Here** from the shortcut menu.

11. Move the following files from **2 Managing Files** to the **Media** folder: **micky&andrew video**, **test sound file** and **training sound file**.

12. Use **Cut** and **Paste** to move the **Sample** folder that is in **My Documents** (not the copy in your folder) to the **ECDL** folder.

Driving Lesson 23 - Selecting Multiple Files

⊞ Park and Read

Often in file management, more than one file at a time needs to be copied, moved or deleted. This means that multiple files need to be selected; there are various ways of doing this.

Ⓡ Manoeuvres

1. View the list of files within the folder **Reports**.

2. View the contents as a list, by selecting **View | List**.

3. To select a range of files, click once on the second file in the list, **Cam**, hold down the <**Shift**> key on the keyboard, then click on the last file in the list, **Cia**. Release the <**Shift**> key. All the files in between will be selected.

4. Click away from the selection to deselect all files.

5. Display the files in the **2 Managing Files** folder and view the contents as a list.

6. To select multiple files that are not in a range, hold down <**Ctrl**> on the keyboard and click on all the files to be selected. Use <**Ctrl**> to select files as in the following diagram.

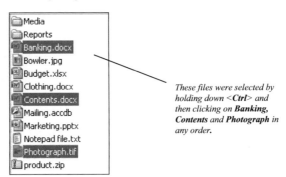

*These files were selected by holding down <**Ctrl**> and then clicking on **Banking**, **Contents** and **Photograph** in any order.*

7. Click away from the selection.

Driving Lesson 23 - Continued

8. To select all the files and folders in the **View** window, select **Edit | Select All**. Click away from the selection.

9. Alternatively, the key press **<Ctrl A>** on the keyboard can be used to select all files. Press **<Ctrl A>** to select all the files.

10. Click anywhere in the **View** pane, away from the selected files, to remove the selection.

11. All the files and folders in the **View** window except for one or two can be easily selected. Select the files not required, e.g. **Bowler** and **Photograph**, (using **<Ctrl>**) then select **Edit | Invert Selection** from the **Menu Bar**. All files apart from the original two will now be selected.

12. Click away from the selection.

13. Once multiple files have been selected, dragging and dropping any one of the selected files will move or copy all the files. Multiple files can also be selected for deletion.

All the instructions in this Driving Lesson and the two previous lessons, which refer to files, apply in <u>exactly</u> the same way to folders. Folders and files can be selected, copied and moved in an identical manner. Mixtures of files and folders can be selected, copied or moved in the same operation.

Driving Lesson 24 - Viewing Object Properties

Park and Read

To view the properties of any object (folder or file), right click on it and select **Properties**. A properties dialog box appears giving information about the **Type**, **Location**, **Size**, when **Created**, **Modified** and the **Attributes** of the object.

Manoeuvres

1. To view the properties of an object, point and right click on it. Right click on the folder **2 Managing Files**.

2. Click **Properties** to display the **Properties** dialog box.

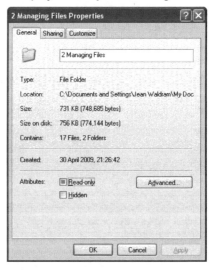

3. Note that the **Contains** value shows the total number of files and other folders within this folder, even if some of those objects are in subfolders.

4. Click on the **Cancel** button to close the dialog box.

5. Right click on any **.docx**, **.pptx** or **.xlsx** file, select **Properties** and view all the information. Click the **Summary** tab, then the **Advanced** button, to see useful statistical information about the file. Return to the **General** tab.

6. If the **Read-only** attribute for a file is set, that file can be opened and read but cannot be amended under its own name; the file is locked. To allow a file to be amended (Read/Write access), this attribute must be unchecked.

> *If the **Read-only** attribute for a folder is set or cleared, there is an option to apply the change to all files and subfolders.*

7. Close the dialog box and close all open windows.

Driving Lesson 25 - Renaming Files and Folders

▣ Park and Read

Files and **Folders** can be renamed to help with their management. Care should be taken not to change file extensions when renaming, as file extensions determine what application is used when a file is opened.

☞ Manoeuvres

1. Open the **My Computer** window and display the **Folders** view.

2. Expand the **My Documents**, **CIA DATA FILES**, **ECDL** and **2 Managing Files** folders within the **C:** drive.

3. Click on the **Media** folder to open it, then click with the **right** mouse button on the **micky&andrew video** icon. A shortcut menu will appear, similar to that below (you will probably have different entries).

4. Select the **Rename** option from the menu.

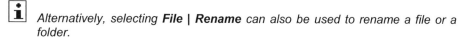 *Alternatively, selecting **File | Rename** can also be used to rename a file or a folder.*

5. The name **micky&andrew video** is now highlighted. Type in **Video file** (if the file extension is displayed add **.avi** after the name). Press **<Enter>**.

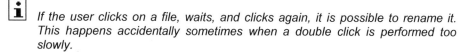 *If the user clicks on a file, waits, and clicks again, it is possible to rename it. This happens accidentally sometimes when a double click is performed too slowly.*

6. Folder names can be changed in a similar way. Change the **Media** folder name to **Video Clips**.

Driving Lesson 26 - Deleting Files and Folders

 Park and Read

Files and folders can be deleted in four main ways:

a. Select the icon by clicking on it, then press the <Delete> key or the **Delete** button on the toolbar (if it has been configured).

b. Click once on the file/folder with the **right** mouse button then select **Delete**.

c. Click and drag the file / folder over the **Recycle Bin** icon on the **Desktop** or the entry in **Folders** view, then release the icon "into" the bin (the Recycle Bin is covered in the next Driving Lesson).

d. Select the file/folder and select **File | Delete** from the menu.

i *The result of deleting a file depends on its location. If the file is deleted from the hard disk, the file is moved to the **Recycle Bin**. If the file is deleted from a floppy disk or portable storage device, then it is deleted permanently.*

Manoeuvres

1. In the **Folders** pane, click on the **Reports** folder, to select it. Press the <Delete> key.

2. A message appears, confirming that the folder and its contents are to be deleted. Select **Yes** and the folder will be removed to the **Recycle Bin**.

3. Click once on the **Notepad file** icon, within the **2 Managing Files** folder with the **right** mouse button, then select **Delete** from the shortcut menu. At the message, select **No**, to keep the file.

4. Click and drag the **Notepad file** icon over the **Recycle Bin** icon in the **Folders** pane and release the mouse button. The icon disappears from the **View** window and the file is deleted (if a **Confirm File Delete** box appears click **Yes**).

5. Delete the **Sample** subfolder from within your own folder in **My Documents** using the **Delete** button, ⊠ on the toolbar. If the button is not present use the **File | Delete** command from the **Menu Bar**.

6. Confirm the deletion, then close the **My Computer** window.

Driving Lesson 27 - The Recycle Bin

🅿 Park and Read

When files or folders are deleted, they are not instantly removed from the hard disk. They are held in the **Recycle Bin**, whose icon can be seen on the **Desktop** (or in **Folders** view). All deleted items are stored there until the **Recycle Bin** is emptied. Until then, the files can be restored. Objects deleted from a floppy disk or other portable devices are **not** held in the **Recycle Bin**, but are deleted instantly.

↱ Manoeuvres

1. The **Recycle Bin** is situated on the **Desktop** and the icon changes according to whether it contains any files, or is empty, .

2. Double click on the **Recycle Bin** icon. The **Recycle Bin** window opens, showing a list of all items that have been deleted. Select **View | Details**.

3. There may be many items listed if the **Recycle Bin** has not been emptied recently but the three most recent items should be those deleted in the last exercise. Click the **Date Deleted** header twice to sort in descending date order if necessary.

Name	Original Location	Date Deleted ▼
🗀 Sample	C:\Documents and Settings\Brian Waldram\My Documents	08/08/2007 21:20
📄 Notepad file.txt	C:\Documents and Settings\Brian Waldram\My Documents\CIA DATA FILES\ECDL\2 Managing Files	08/08/2007 21:20
🗀 Reports	C:\Documents and Settings\Brian Waldram\My Documents\CIA DATA FILES\ECDL\2 Managing Files	08/08/2007 21:19

4. Click **Notepad file** to select it, then either select **File | Restore** from the menu or click [🔁 Restore this item] from the **Recycle Bin Tasks** area (a confirmation may be required). The file is removed from the **Recycle Bin** and placed where it was before deletion. If the folder that contained the file has also been deleted, the **Recycle Bin** recreates the folder in which to place the file.

5. Restore the **Reports** folder in a similar manner then close the **Recycle Bin** window.

6. Click with the **right** mouse button on the **Recycle Bin** icon.

7. From the shortcut menu, select **Empty Recycle Bin** (if there are no files in the **Recycle Bin**, this option is not available). A confirmation message appears.

> Open
> Explore
> Empty Recycle Bin
> Create Shortcut
> Properties

8. Clicking **Yes** would permanently remove all contents of the **Recycle Bin**. To protect documents from deletion, select **No** at this time.

9. Display the contents of the **ECDL** folder and delete the **Sample** folder, within, to send it to the **Recycle Bin**.

Driving Lesson 28 - Copy a Floppy Disk

▣ Park and Read

Important files can be **copied** to a floppy disk as described earlier, in case of a hard drive failure. This lesson describes how to make a copy of a floppy disk.

⌒ Manoeuvres

1.　If your computer does not have a floppy disk drive or you do not have a floppy disk containing some data and a blank floppy disk to copy to then read this for information only, then progress to the next Driving Lesson.

2.　Open the **My Computer** window. Check the contents of a floppy disk in drive **A** to make sure that it contains data files.

3.　**Right click** on the **(A:)** drive icon, then select **Copy Disk**.

4.　The **Copy Disk** dialog box appears.

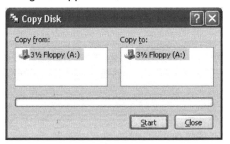

5.　To start the operation, click on the **Start** button. A prompt to insert the source disk appears.

6.　Insert the floppy disk to copy, if not already in the drive and click **OK**.

7.　The contents of the floppy disk are now read and a prompt to insert the destination disk appears.

8.　**Remove** the source disk and **insert** the destination disk. Click **OK**.

9.　The contents of the source disk are now copied to the destination disk. An exact copy is created. Any original data on the destination disk is lost.

10.　Select **Close** when completed.

11.　Close **My Computer** and remove the floppy disk from the drive.

Driving Lesson 29 - Searching for Files/Folders

▣ Park and Read

Not too long after purchasing the computer the user will probably have a large number of files stored in a variety of folders. It can become difficult to remember where every file is stored (this is where a well designed folder system is essential). If you cannot find a file, *Windows* has the ability to search for a required file or folder based on several criteria.

Search Options can be used to narrow down the search. All files that match the set criteria will be listed with their locations. Searches can be made on partial file names or on file content, e.g. words in a document.

☞ Manoeuvres

1. Select the **Start** button, then **Search,** [🔍 Search].

2. Select [➡ All files and folders] from the **Search Companion** options.

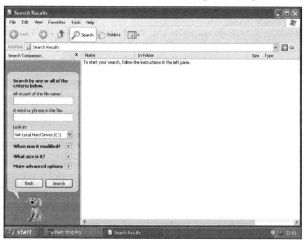

3. Click in the **All or part of the file name** box and enter **ECDL**.

4. Make sure the **Look in** box shows **Local Hard Drives (C:)** and click the **Search** button.

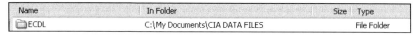

Name	In Folder	Size	Type
📁 ECDL	C:\My Documents\CIA DATA FILES		File Folder

5. The **ECDL** folder will be found and details shown on the right. Make sure **View | Details** is selected. The actual path to the data may be different.

Driving Lesson 29 - Continued

6. By default the search word can be found anywhere in the name of the file or folder. Click ⬚ Back ⬚, in the **Search Companion** pane, then in the **All or part of the file name** box overtype **ECDL** with the text **video**.

7. Click on the drop down arrow to the right of the **Look in** box, select **Browse** and locate and select the **2 Managing Files** folder in the **ECDL** folder, within **My Documents** and click **OK**.

8. Click the **Search** button. The **2 Managing Files** folder will now be searched for any objects that have **video** in their name. After a couple of seconds, the search results should appear in the main part of the screen.

Name	In Folder	Size	Type
📁 Video Clips	C:\My Documents\CIA DATA FILES\ECDL\2 Managing Files		File Folder
▶ Video file.avi	C:\My Documents\CIA DATA FILES\ECDL\2 Managing Files\Video Clips	115 KB	AVI File

9. Wildcards may be used in the search. Click ⬚ Back ⬚, clear the **All or part of the file name** box and enter **m***. This will search for names that begin with **m** followed by any number of other characters. Click **Search**.

Name	In Folder	Size	Type
📄 Mailing.accdb	C:\My Documents\CIA DATA FILES\ECDL\2 Managing Files	292 KB	Microsoft Access..
📄 Marketing.pptx	C:\My Documents\CIA DATA FILES\ECDL\2 Managing Files	79 KB	Microsoft PowerP.

ℹ️ *This is different to searching just for **m**. That search would find all objects that contained the character **m** anywhere in the name.*

10. Searches can be made based on content. Click ⬚ Back ⬚, clear the **All or part of the file name** box and enter **sales** in the **A word or phrase in the file** box. This will search for any file that has the word **sales** in the content. Click **Search**.

Name	In Folder	Size	Type
📊 Budget.xlsx	C:\My Documents\CIA DATA FILES\ECDL\2 Managing Files	10 KB	Microsoft Excel ...
📄 Marketing.pptx	C:\My Documents\CIA DATA FILES\ECDL\2 Managing Files	79 KB	Microsoft PowerP.

11. All search criteria can be combined to form more complex searches. Click ⬚ Back ⬚, leave the **sales** criteria and enter **m*** in the **All or part of the file name** box. This will search for files beginning with **m** that contain the word **sales**.

12. Click **Search**. Only the **Marketing.pptx** file is found.

13. Change the entry in the **Look in** box to point to the **ECDL** folder and practise searching for files there.

14. Clear the criteria boxes in the **Search Companion** pane, leave **ECDL** in the **Look in** box and leave the **Search Results** window open.

Driving Lesson 30 - Advanced Searching

P Park and Read

More advanced searches can be performed in *Windows*. It is possible to search for files of a certain size or type, or those which have been modified on or between specific dates.

Manoeuvres

1. With the **Search Results** window open and **ECDL** in the **Look in** box, click the | When was it modified? | link.

2. Select **Specify dates** and enter the dates **01/01/2007** and **31/12/2007** in the **from** and **to** date fields respectively.

3. Click **Search**. Scroll down the list to view the results.

4. Click **Back** and change **Modified Date** to **Created Date** in the drop down list. Change the search criteria to **Within the past year**; this will search for files created or modified recently. Click **Search**.

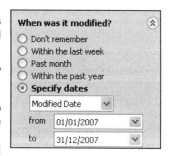

5. Searches can be made based on file size. Click **Back**, cancel the date search by selecting the **Don't remember** option, then scroll down and click the | What size is it? | link.

6. Click the **Specify size (in KB)** option. Set the criteria to **at least** and the size to **100**.

7. Click **Search** to see all files in the **ECDL** folder that are **100 KB** or more.

8. Click **Back** and cancel the size search by selecting the **Don't remember** option.

9. Searches can be made based on file type. Click the **More advanced options** link and expand the drop down list for **Type of file**.

10. Scroll down and select **JPEG Image**. Click **Search** to see all that type of file in the **ECDL** folder.

11. Click **Back** and cancel the file type search by selecting **(All Files and Folders)** from the **Type of file** drop down list.

12. Close the **Search Results** window.

Driving Lesson 31 - Revision

This Driving Lesson covers the features introduced in this section. Try not to refer to the previous Driving Lessons while completing it.

1. Obtain a floppy disk or any other portable storage device.

2. Create a backup copy of the files in the **Reports** folder to the floppy disk or another storage device.

3. Create a subfolder within your own named folder (in **My Documents**) and name it **Organisation**.

4. Copy the **Advert** and **CIA Training Ltd - Overview** files from **Reports** into the **Organisation** folder.

5. **Advert** was copied in error. Check that **Advert** is still in the **Reports** folder then delete it from the **Organisation** folder.

6. Open the **Organisation** folder and rename the **CIA Training Ltd - Overview** as **CIA Background.docx**.

7. Delete your folder (your name) and all of its contents.

8. Delete the **Photograph** file from **2 Managing Files**.

9. **Photograph** has been deleted in error. Restore it from the **Recycle Bin** to its original location.

10. View the **Properties** of **Photograph**. What is shown as the **Modified** date?

11. Find any **Microsoft Word Document** files in **My Documents** that contain the text **sewing machine**. What is the name of the file?

12. Close the **Search** dialog box.

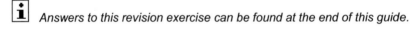 *Answers to this revision exercise can be found at the end of this guide.*

If you experienced any difficulty completing this exercise refer back to the Driving Lessons in this section. Then redo the Revision Exercise.

Driving Lesson 32 - Revision

This Driving Lesson covers the features introduced in this section. Try not to refer to the previous Driving Lessons while completing it.

1. Somewhere within the **ECDL** folder are files that have information on advertising. Search the folder for any file containing the text '**advertising**'. One of the files should be from the **Managing Files** folder. What is the name and type of the relevant file?

2. Create a new folder within the supplied **ECDL** folder and call it **Revision**.

3. Search the **2 Managing Files** folder for all files that are of the type **Microsoft Office Word; Document** (<u>not</u> Microsoft Word Document).

4. Select all the files from the **Search** dialog box and use **Edit | Copy** to copy them all.

5. Close the **Search** dialog box and open the new **Revision** folder. Use **Edit | Paste** to add the copied files to the folder.

6. Copy all the files within **Revision** so as to produce duplicates within the same folder. How many files are in the folder?

7. Search for all the files in **2 Managing Files** that are at least **100Kb**, and copy them to the **Revision** folder. How many files are now in the folder?

8. Delete the folder **Revision** including all its contents.

9. Close any open windows.

 *Answers to this revision exercise can be found at the end of this guide.*

If you experienced any difficulty completing this exercise. refer back to the Driving Lessons in this section. Then redo the Revision Exercise.

Once you are confident with the features, complete the Record of Achievement Matrix referring to the section at the end of the guide. Only when competent move on to the next Section.

Section 3
Print Management

By the end of this Section you should be able to:

Select a Printer

Set a Default Printer

Add a New Printer

View a Print Job

Control Print Jobs

Understand how to Perform Maintenance

To gain an understanding of the above features, work through the **Driving Lessons** in this **Section**.

For each **Driving Lesson**, read the **Park and Read** instructions, without touching the keyboard, then work through the numbered steps of the **Manoeuvres** on the computer. Complete the **Revision Exercise(s)** at the end of the section to test your knowledge.

Driving Lesson 33 - Printers

▣ Park and Read

The **Printers and Faxes** window contains icons for each installed printer that is available to the computer, either via a network connection or directly connected. A properties dialog box can be displayed for each printer allowing various settings for the printer to be changed. If more than one printer is available, it is possible to change the default printer.

It is also possible to add a new printer to the selection available. Clicking the **Add Printer** icon starts the **Add Printer Wizard**, which guides the user through the process of setting up a new printer.

Double clicking on a specific printer's icon displays the **print queue** window for that printer. This window gives information regarding the print jobs that have been sent to that printer and the progress of each job.

⌐ Manoeuvres

1.   Click **Start** and select **Printers and Faxes** from the **Start Menu**.

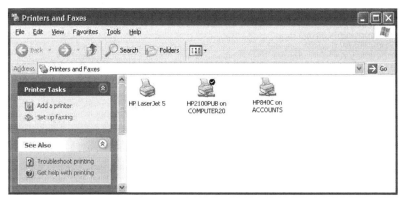

Your printer/s will be different to those shown in the diagram

ℹ️ *Alternatively this window can be displayed by clicking the **Printers and Faxes** icon in the **Control Panel** window.*

2.   This example shows one directly connected printer (**HP LaserJet 5**) and two network printers available. Notice that the icons are slightly different for the network printers. A shared attached printer will also include a hand,

   e.g. .

Driving Lesson 33 - Continued

3.   The tick next to the printer icon indicates that this is currently defined as the default printer for the system. To make a different printer the default, right click on its icon and select **Set as Default Printer** from the shortcut menu.

4.   Right click on any printer icon and select **Properties** from the shortcut menu.

An example of a printer properties dialog box

*The tabs available in the **Properties** dialog box will depend on the type of printer selected.*

5.   There are a number of tabs at the top of the **Properties** dialog box, which allow different aspects of the printer operation to be changed. **General** gives general information about the printer. The **Printing Preferences** button on this tab allows features such as paper orientation and size to be controlled. The other tabs control all other aspects associated with the printer, e.g. **Sharing**. Examine the options available then close the dialog box.

6.   Double click on any of the printer icons to open the **print queue** window, listing all current print jobs for that printer.

7.   Close the **print queue** window.

8.   If possible, ensure that a directly connected printer is defined as the default printer.

9.   Leave the **Printers and Faxes** window open for the next Driving Lesson.

Driving Lesson 34 - Add a New Printer

 Park and Read

If a new printer is made available, its details must be added to the computer before it can be used. An **Add Printer** wizard is available to make the task easier. *Windows XP* also has a powerful auto-detect system (Plug and Play) which will detect and add the details for most printers automatically. *Windows* will automatically add details for a local printer connected using a USB port.

Manoeuvres

These actions can be read for information now but should only be followed when a new printer is connected or the icon for an existing printer is lost.

1. Click the **Add a printer** icon under **Printer Tasks** to start the **Add Printer Wizard**.

2. Click **Next** on the **Welcome** screen, then indicate whether the printer is **Local** (attached directly) or connected via a **Network**.

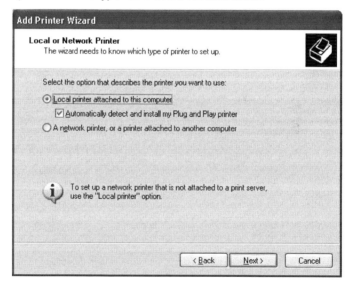

3. If a **Local printer** is selected, check the **Automatically detect...** option and click **Next**. If the system recognises the printer model and finds the software to control it (driver software), the process is automatic. Most common printers should be able to be detected in this manner, if not go to step 5.

Driving Lesson 34 - Continued

4. Click **Next** at the next screen and then **Finish**. A new icon will be added to the **Printers** window.

5. If the **Automatically detect…** option is not selected or does not work, the wizard screens will have to be completed manually. From the **Local or Network Printer** screen (shown above), do not select the **Automatically detect option**. Click **Next** to move to the next screen.

6. For a **Local** printer, select the port the printer is connected to, (usually **LPT1**). Click **Next**. Select the **Manufacturer and model** of your printer. If the **Drivers** for the printer are on a disk, click **Have Disk** and follow the instructions. Click **Next**. Go to step 8.

i   *See the **Printer Maintenance** Driving Lesson for more information about installing and updating printer drivers.*

7. For a **Network** printer, enter the path of an existing printer in the appropriate box or click the option to find one by browsing. Click **Next**, (if the browsing option was chosen click **Next** again after finding the required printer).

8. Enter a name for the printer. This is the name that appears with the printer icon and identifies this printer whenever printer selection is required. Click **Next**.

9. Select a sharing option (the default is not to share) and click **Next**.

10. Request a test page, if required, and click **Next**.

11. Click **Finish** from the **Summary** screen and a new icon will be added to the **Printers** window.

12. Leave the **Printers and Faxes** window open for the next Driving Lesson.

Driving Lesson 35 - Print Jobs

▣ Park and Read

It is possible to view and control the status of a print job.

⌇ Manoeuvres

1. From the **Printers** window, double click on the icon of the printer to be viewed. The **print queue** is displayed.

There will be no items in the queue if no print jobs are currently being processed.

Depending on the system being used you may not be allowed to control the printer. This is most likely to happen with a networked printer. In this case the rest of this exercise should be read for information.

2. To demonstrate controlling print jobs on this screen it will be convenient to temporarily pause the printer operation. Select **Printer** from the **Menu Bar** in the **print queue** window and click on **Pause Printing**. The word **Paused** should appear on the **Title Bar**.

3. To quickly create a print job, first display the contents of the **2 Managing Files** folder in the **My Documents** window.

4. Right click on **Notepad file** and select **Print** from the shortcut menu. Close the **Managing Files** window.

5. Redisplay the **print queue** window and in a few seconds a print job will appear. It will stay there because the printer operation has been paused.

Driving Lesson 35 - Continued

i *If the printer is not paused, the job will print and be removed from the queue almost immediately.*

6.   Note the information about the print job that is displayed.

7.   As well as controlling the printer, individual print jobs can be controlled from this window.

8.   Click on the **Notepad file** job to select it, then select **Document** from the menu bar.

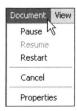

9.   Select **Pause** from the menu. The status of the job changes to **Paused**. If the printer was active, printing of this job would stop and the next print job on the queue would be printed.

10.   With the **Notepad file** still highlighted, select **Document** again. Select **Resume** and the job would resume printing from where it paused.

11.   With the **Notepad file** still highlighted, select **Document | Restart**. If the printer was active, printing of this job would start again from the beginning.

12.   With the **Notepad file** still highlighted, select **Document | Cancel**. Click **Yes** to confirm the action. The print job is permanently removed from the queue. A job can be cancelled if it is waiting in the queue or currently printing. Cancelling a job that is printing will terminate the print and allow any subsequent jobs in the queue to start.

i *Some printers have an internal memory which stores currently printing pages, so that sometimes printing can still continue for a time after a job is cancelled.*

13.   To reactivate the printer, select **Printer** from the menu bar in the **print queue** window and click on **Pause Printing** so that the tick is removed. The word **Paused** will disappear from the title bar to confirm that the printer is active again.

i *All jobs can be removed from the print queue by selecting **Printer | Cancel All Documents**. This is sometimes known as **purging** print jobs.*

14.   Close the **print queue**.

15.   Leave the **Printers and Faxes** window open.

Driving Lesson 36 - Printer Maintenance

Park and Read

There are various maintenance tasks that will need to be performed from time to time when you use a printer. You will probably need to align ink cartridges after installing or replacing one, but you may also need to do this if printed characters are improperly formed, or are misaligned at the left margin, or when vertical, straight lines look wavy. You may need to print a test page to check if a printer is printing text and graphics correctly. A test page also shows information such as the printer name, model and driver software version, which can help you troubleshoot printer problems. With a new printer, the driver may need installing, or updating in an older printer.

Other tasks that you will probably have to deal with include replacing consumables, such as paper and toner cartridges, and possibly clearing a paper jam. Basic instructions for these tasks are given below - you <u>may</u> need to refer to manufacturer's guidelines.

To print a test page

Click the **Start** button and open the **Control Panel**. Select **Printers and Faxes**. Right click on your printer and select **Properties**. On the **General** tab, look toward the bottom of the dialog box. Click Print Test Page and your printer will automatically print it for you.

To align cartridges

Click the **Start** button and open the **Control Panel**. Select **Printers and Faxes**. Right click on your printer and select **Printing Preferences**. There will be an option on one of the tabs to **Align Print Cartridge** or **Print Head Alignment**, or something similar. Choose this option and follow the instructions given. If you have just installed a new cartridge, you may be prompted to align automatically.

To replace paper

In a laser printer, slide out the paper drawer, insert the new paper (normally under a metal guard and push the drawer back in. Inkjet printers will normally just need paper inserting in the top or the front.

Driving Lesson 36 - Continued

To replace a toner cartridge

If you use a laser printer and the quality isn't as good as it used to be, you may need to replace the toner cartridge. Open the printer door and lift up the hand hold, then remove the old toner cartridge. Get the new cartridge out of the box and give it a gentle shake. Take off the protective tape. Insert the new cartridge, pushing down to ensure it's properly in place.

To clear a paper jam

A paper jam is indicated by a flashing warning light on the printer. First, turn the printer off and on again to see if this will clear the jam. If not, turn the printer off. Remove the paper trays and check for damaged paper. Open any doors, i.e. toner/ink and if necessary remove the toner or ink cartridge to check for paper stuck behind them. Remove any jammed paper by pulling firmly but gently, so it doesn't tear. If it does tear, try turning the rollers to free the paper. Replace paper trays and toner or ink cartridges if they've been removed, close any open doors and turn on the printer. If the paper jam light is still flashing, repeat the process.

To install and update printer drivers

A driver is software that allows a computer to control a printer. Some drivers are included in *Windows*, others are installed when you install the printer. Sometimes you'll need to install drivers using the CD that came with the printer. If there is no CD, go to the printer manufacturer's website and download and install the drivers from there. To install the driver, open the **Control Panel** and double click the **System** icon. Select the **Device Manager** tab. Find the printer for which you want to update the driver and click on it. Select **Properties** and the **Driver** tab. Click **Update Driver**; a dialog box will appear to help you through the process. Select **Display a list of drivers...** then select **Have Disk** and locate the driver file you've downloaded. Select the **.INF** file and click **OK**. You'll need to restart the computer to complete the installation.

Driving Lesson 37 - Revision

· This Driving Lesson covers the features introduced in this section. Try not to refer to the previous Driving Lessons while completing it.

1. The **Printers** window should still be open. If not, open it.

2. View the **Properties** for the default printer. What paper size is currently selected? Cancel the **Properties** box.

3. How do you change the default printer?

4. Use the **Search** feature in **Help** to find information on **printing**.

5. Display the topic **Changing printing preferences** and print a copy of it.

6. Close **Help**.

7. Display the **print queue** for each printer in the **Printers** window in turn. Are there any current jobs?

8. Close any open **print queue** and **Printers** windows.

9. When might you need to align print cartridges?

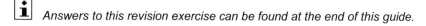

Answers to this revision exercise can be found at the end of this guide.

If you experienced any difficulty completing the Revision, refer back to the Driving Lessons in this section. Then redo the Revision.

Once you are confident with the features, complete the Record of Achievement Matrix referring to the section at the end of the guide. Only when competent move on to the next Section.

Section 4
Running Applications

By the end of this Section you should be able to:

Start and Close an Application

Enter Text

Save and Print Information

Capture Screen Images

Install and Remove Applications

Switch Between Applications

Create and Use Desktop Icons

To gain an understanding of the above features, work through the **Driving Lessons** in this **Section**.

For each **Driving Lesson**, read the **Park and Read** instructions, without touching the keyboard, then work through the numbered steps of the **Manoeuvres** on the computer. Complete the **Revision Exercise(s)** at the end of the section to test your knowledge.

Driving Lesson 38 - Run an Application

▣ Park and Read

When a program is installed on the computer, it normally adds itself somewhere into the **Start** button menus. It may add a new item under **Programs**, or join in with another group of files.

☞ Manoeuvres

1. Select **Start | All Programs | Accessories | WordPad**. This application is a simple word processor. Documents can be opened, edited, formatted, printed, saved and used by other word processors.

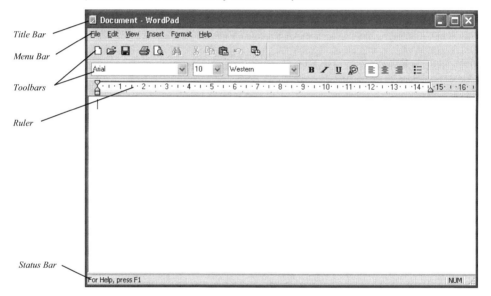

2. The **Title Bar** across the top of the window displays the application name and the current open file, **Document** by default.

3. *WordPad* has a **Menu Bar** across the top of the screen. Beneath this there are two sets of toolbars, (the **Standard** and **Formatting** bars).

4. There is a **Ruler** along the top of the document and a **Status Bar** along the bottom.

5. If any are not visible, then select **View** and select the appropriate option.

Driving Lesson 38 - Continued

6. Click the first menu item, **File**. Take note of the available options.

7. Browse through the other menu options.

8. Note that as the mouse pointer is moved over a menu command a short description of the command appears at the bottom of the window, in the **Status Bar**.

9. Close any open menu by clicking on the screen away from the menu.

10. Move the mouse pointer over any of the buttons on the **Toolbar**, and leave it for a second or two. A **ToolTip** appears, with a longer description of the button in the **Status Bar**.

11. Select **Help | Help Topics** to display the help system.

12. Browse through the help system to understand the capabilities of *WordPad*.

13. Close the **Help** window by clicking the **Close** button, ⊠.

14. Leave *WordPad* open for the next Driving Lesson.

Driving Lesson 39 - Entering & Formatting Text

Park and Read

WordPad uses a flashing cursor to show where the text is entered and edited. The cursor can be moved by clicking the mouse pointer or by using the cursor (arrow) keys on the keyboard. Text is entered at the cursor position and has wordwrap, so that when the edge of the paper is reached, the text automatically wraps on to the next line.

Text can be formatted in a number of ways. Formatting can be done before entering the text, in which case the format is chosen first, or after entering text, when the relevant text is selected and then formatted.

The font, font style, size and colour of text can be changed either by selecting **Format | Font** and selecting from the dialog box, or by using the **Font**, **Font Size**, **Bold**, **Italic**, **Underline** and **Colour** buttons on the **Formatting Toolbar**.

Manoeuvres

1.   Enter the following text into *WordPad*:

      CIA Training Ltd is a specialist publishing company, based in the North East of England. It has been trading for over twenty years and has recently moved to new, larger premises in Sunderland.

      The company is involved in the production of computer training materials. More details are available by telephoning (0191) 549 5002.

2.   Select the first sentence, beginning **CIA Training Ltd**, by clicking and dragging the mouse pointer over the text, so that it is highlighted.

3.   Press <**Delete**> to remove the text.

4.   To cancel the deletion, select **Edit | Undo** from the menu.

5.   Click after **larger premises in Sunderland.** and type in **These premises are located within the Business and Innovation Centre on the north bank of the River Wear.**

6.   Select the first sentence again, then locate the **Font** drop down list using **Tooltips**. Click it and choose a different font.

7.   In a similar manner, change the size, font style (bold, italic or underline) and colour of the selected text.

8.   Practise formatting text, both before and after entering the text then leave *WordPad* open for the next Driving Lesson.

Driving Lesson 40 - Saving Text

🅿 Park and Read

Documents created in *WordPad* can be saved on to the hard disk or any other storage media to be used again. *WordPad* can only have one document open at a time, so any open document will be closed before another is opened. If the document has not been saved there will be a prompt to save it then.

Manoeuvres

1. To save the document select **File | Save** (alternatively, click the **Save** button, ⊟ or press <**Ctrl S**>).

2. The **Save in** box at the top of the **Save As** dialog box displays **My Documents**. Double click on **CIA DATA FILES**, **ECDL**, then **2 Managing Files** folder and then the **Reports** folder. The contents of the **Reports** folder will be shown on the right.

3. From **Save as type** make sure **Rich Text Format (RTF)** is selected and enter the **File name** as **WordPad Document**. Click the **Save** button to save this file to the specified folder.

4. Change the text **CIA** to **ABC** then select the **Open** button, 📂, (alternatively, press <**Ctrl O**> or select **File | Open**).

5. Check that the **2 Managing Files** folder is being displayed, use the **Up One Level** button, 📁, then change the file type to **All Documents**. Click on the file **Notepad file**.

6. Click on the **Open** button. There will be a prompt to save the changes to the original document. Click **No** to ignore the changes. The document that was open is now closed automatically.

7. **Notepad file** will now be opened and visible on screen. Use formatting tools to change the appearance of the document.

8. Place a blank floppy disk in the disk drive or attach a storage device, select **File | Save As**. As formatting has been applied, the file must be saved as **rtf** type.

9. Change the **File name** to **Cia2**, the **Save as type** to **Rich Text Format** and the location to a portable storage device. Click **Save**.

10. Leave the document open for the next Driving Lesson.

Driving Lesson 41 - Print a Document

🅿 Park and Read

It is an easy task to print out documents from *WordPad*. The printing margins can be set from the **Page Setup** dialog box. Page layout can be previewed before printing within **Print Preview**. A picture of the printed page will appear, along with the margins that have been set.

Manoeuvres

1. With **Banking2** open, select **File | Page Setup**.

2. Select the **Size** as **A4** and change all the margins to **50mm**. Click **OK** when finished.

3. Click the **Print Preview** button, 🔍.

4. Click the **Zoom In** button to take a closer look.

ℹ️ *If the document runs to more than one page then **Next Page** and **Prev Page** can be used. **Two Page** shows two pages of the document at once.*

5. Click the **Print** button, Print....

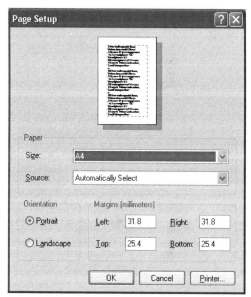

ℹ️ *Alternatively, from the normal view, select **File | Print** or press **<Ctrl P>**.*

6. Select to print **1** copy of **All** pages. Check that your printer is set up, connected and on-line. Click **Print**.

ℹ️ *Alternatively clicking the **Print** button, 🖶, prints one copy of the document to the default printer.*

7. Use **Page Setup** to set all margins to **25mm**.

8. Leave the document open.

Driving Lesson 42 - Using Print Screen

🅿 Park and Read

An image of any screen display can be captured using the **Print Screen** button then used in another application. For example a screen image (sometimes called a screen shot, or screen dump) can be added to a document in a word processing application and then printed out. Moving images on a screen will not be captured.

Manoeuvres

1. Minimise the *WordPad* window and use **My Computer** to display the contents of the **Local Disk (C:)**.

2. Press <**Print Screen**>, found at the top right of the keyboard. This stores an image of the current screen in an area of the computer known as the **Clipboard**.

ℹ️ *Capture an image of an active window by holding down <**Alt**> while pressing <**Print Screen**>.*

3. Close the **Local Disk (C:)** display and click on the **Banking2 - WordPad** button on the **Taskbar** to redisplay the *WordPad* screen.

4. Click the **New** button, 🗋, to start a new document. Select a document type of **Rich Text Document** when prompted and click **OK**.

5. The current document is automatically closed. If a **Save changes...** message appears, select **No**.

6. At the top of the new document, type the line **This shows the contents of my Hard Disk**. Press <**Enter**> to start a new line.

7. Click the **Paste** button, 📋. The recently captured screen image is pasted into the document, but it is too large.

8. Scroll up so the top left corner of the image can be seen. If the image is selected there will be a small square "handle" there (if not, click once on the image).

9. Click and drag this handle diagonally down and right for a few centimetres to reduce the size of the image until it fits on a single page.

10. Select **File | Page Setup** and select **Landscape** as the **Orientation**. Click **OK**.

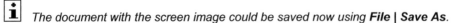

11. Select **File | Print** and request to print **1** copy of **All** pages. Check that your printer is set up and connected. Click **Print**. The image may be printed on a separate page to the text.

ℹ️ *The document with the screen image could be saved now using **File | Save As**.*

12. Leave *WordPad* open for the next Driving Lesson.

Driving Lesson 43 - Switch between Applications

 Park and Read

More than one application can be running at the same time. The **Taskbar** shows the applications currently running.

Manoeuvres

1. Click ▬ to minimise the *WordPad* window.

2. Select **Start | All Programs | Accessories | Calculator**. The **Calculator** accessory opens.

> *There are two different views of the calculator, **Scientific** and **Standard**. Select the required view by clicking **View** on the menu and selecting the appropriate menu choice. The calculator can be operated by clicking on the buttons with the mouse, or by using the keyboard.*

3. Look at the **Taskbar**. It shows the last *WordPad* document is still open in the background.

4. Click on the **Document - WordPad** button on the **Taskbar**. Now *WordPad* becomes the active window (the **Title Bar** becomes blue).

5. Click the **Restore Down** button, 🗗. The button is replaced by the **Maximize** button, 🗖.

6. The application is now displayed in a smaller window. The sizing and scaling techniques used and practised earlier apply to all windows. Reduce the size of the window by clicking and dragging the bottom right corner.

7. Click the **Maximise** button to change the window back to its full size.

8. Now click on **Calculator** on the **Taskbar**.

9. The diagram in the next Driving Lesson shows the **Standard Calculator**, if the **Scientific Calculator** is displayed, select **View | Standard**.

10. Experiment. Try a few calculations. Use both the mouse and keyboard.

11. Select **View | Scientific**. Try a few more calculations in this new mode then select **View | Standard** again.

12. The *WordPad* window can still be seen, even though it's not the active window. Click once on the *WordPad* window to make it active.

13. Leave both applications open.

Driving Lesson 44 - Closing an Application

▣ Park and Read

Applications shown on the **Taskbar** by a button are still open. To remove an application it must be closed. There are various methods to close down an active application.

Sometimes however an application can become 'stuck' and not respond to any of its buttons or commands. In such an emergency there is a way that *Windows* can close the application down.

⟳ Manoeuvres

1. Make **Calculator** the active window by clicking its button on the **Taskbar**.

2. Close the **Calculator** by clicking the **Close** button (top right).

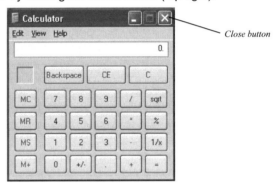

Close button

3. *WordPad* is brought to the front and displayed.

ⓘ *Another method to close down an application is to use **File | Exit** from the menu where this is available.*

4. Assuming that *WordPad* needs to be shut down but is not responding to the **Close** button or the **File | Exit** command, right click on a blank area of the **Taskbar** and select **Task Manager** from the shortcut menu. Alternatively, press and hold down <**Ctrl Alt**> and then press <**Delete**>.

5. The **Windows Task Manager** window appears. Make sure the **Applications** tab is selected. All current applications are listed.

6. Select the **WordPad** task and click **End Task**. The application will be shut down.

ⓘ *This method must NOT be used as a normal close down method. Data in use may be corrupted or lost.*

7. Close the **Windows Task Manager** window.

Driving Lesson 45 - Install/Uninstall an Application

 Park and Read

Most *Windows* applications include programs that will control their installation process automatically. The user may then have to select from menu options and will usually have to make choices from a series of Wizard screens. These will typically ask where the application is to be installed and maybe what optional features are required. When the screens are completed, the application will be installed. *Windows XP* can also handle manual program installation and removal by the use of an **Add or Remove Programs** feature.

 Manoeuvres

1.   Place the required application CD/DVD or floppy in the appropriate drive. If the disk has an **Autorun** feature, the installation program will run automatically. If not, open the **My Computer** window then double click on **Control Panel**.

[i]   *Some applications can now be downloaded directly from providers using the Internet.*

2.   Double click the **Add or Remove Programs** icon, to display the **Add or Remove Programs** window.

3.   By default the window is shown in **Change or Remove Programs** mode and displays a list of installed applications. Click **Add New Programs**.

4.   Click the **CD or Floppy** button and click **Next**. If *Windows* cannot find the installation program, use the **Browse** button to search for it manually on the appropriate drive. The name of the program, e.g. **setup.exe**, will usually be given with the installation instructions.

5.   When the program name is displayed in the **Open** box, click **Finish.** The installation program will run. Answer any queries and follow the instructions until the application is installed.

6.   To remove an application, display the **Add or Remove Programs** window as before and make sure **Change or Remove Programs** is selected.

7.   Click on the required application to select it and display some further information, then click on the **Change/Remove** button.

8.   Depending on the application, it may be removed immediately (after a confirmation prompt), or there may be more choices to select. Answer any queries and follow the instructions until the application is removed.

9.   Close any open windows or dialog boxes.

Driving Lesson 46 - Create Desktop Icons

▣ Park and Read

Icons called **Shortcuts** can be easily created on the **Desktop**. A **Shortcut** is rather like a "sign post" which points to an object which is in a different place. A commonly used file may be hidden in a folder many layers down on the hard disk, requiring many mouse clicks to get to it. A shortcut to this file may be created and placed in a convenient place, such as on the **Desktop** itself. When the shortcut icon is clicked, the file is opened immediately. Shortcuts may point to files, folders or programs.

☞ Manoeuvres

1. To create a shortcut for the **Calculator**, select **Start | All Programs | Accessories**.

2. Move the mouse over **Calculator** and right click. From the shortcut menu, select **Send To**, then **Desktop (create shortcut)**.

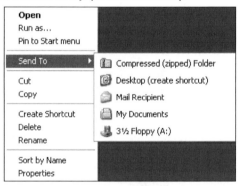

3. Click anywhere on a clear part of the **Desktop** to remove the menus.

4. A new icon appears on the **Desktop**, . Double click on it to start the **Calculator** application.

5. Close the **Calculator** window.

6. To delete the shortcut, right click on the **Calculator** icon on the **Desktop** and select **Delete**, then **Yes**.

Driving Lesson 46 - Continued

7. Shortcuts can be created to any folder or file. In **My Computer**, expand the **My Documents**, **CIA DATA FILES** and **ECDL** folders in the **Folders** pane.

8. Right click **2 Managing Files**. From the shortcut menu, select **Send To**, then **Desktop (create shortcut)**.

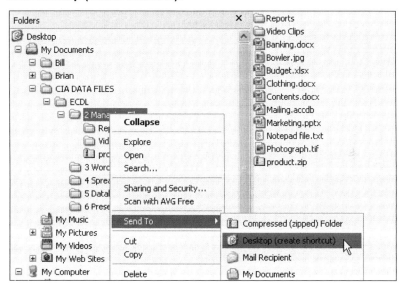

9. Close the **My Computer** window to see the **Desktop**. A new folder icon has appeared on the **Desktop**, ![Shortcut to 2 Managing Files]. Right click the icon and select **Rename** from the menu.

10. Type **Course Data** and press <**Enter**> to replace the highlighted name.

11. Double click the icon to open the folder and display the contents.

12. Right click **Notepad file** and from the shortcut menu, select **Send To**, then **Desktop (create shortcut)**.

13. Close the folder display.

14. A new file icon appears on the **Desktop**, ![Shortcut to Notepad file.txt]. The appearance of a file icon depends on what type of file it is. Using file icons is covered in the next Driving Lesson.

Driving Lesson 47 - Use Desktop Icons

▣ Park and Read

Double clicking on an icon for a program will start that program.

Double clicking on an icon for a folder will open that folder.

Double clicking on an icon for a file will start an application that will open that file. The application that starts depends on the type of file, which is defined by the file extension. So for example double clicking an icon for a **.docx** file will start *Word*, double clicking an icon for a **.xlsx** file will start *Excel*. This is why it is important to maintain the correct file extensions when copying or renaming files.

If *Windows* does not know which application to use to open a file, it will offer to look it up on the Web or prompt the user to select one from a list such as this:

⟲ Manoeuvres

1. Double click on the **Shortcut to Notepad file** icon created in the last Driving Lesson. The **Notepad** application will start and **Notepad file** will be opened ready for editing or other processes.

2. Close the **Notepad** application.

3. Create shortcut icons for other files in the **2 Managing Files** folder and double click them to see which applications start.

4. Use right click and **Delete** to remove all the shortcut icons created in both this Driving Lesson and the last one.

Driving Lesson 48 - Revision

This Driving Lesson covers the features introduced in this section. Try not to refer to the previous Driving Lessons while completing it.

1.   Create a **Desktop** shortcut to the **Paint** accessory.

2.   Create a **Desktop** shortcut to the **WordPad** accessory.

3.   Rename the **Paint** shortcut to **Drawing**.

4.   Use the shortcuts to open both applications.

5.   Practise switching between them using the **Taskbar**.

6.   In **WordPad** create a small letter inviting a friend to a party.

7.   Print the letter.

8.   Save the letter in **My Documents** as **Party**.

9.   Close the letter.

10.   Close both open applications.

11.   Remove both shortcuts from the **Desktop**.

If you experienced any difficulty completing this exercise, refer back to the Driving Lessons in this section. Then redo the Revision Exercise.

Once you are confident with the features, complete the Record of Achievement Matrix referring to the section at the end of the guide. Only when competent move on to the next Section.

Section 5
Using Compress

By the end of this Section you should be able to:

Understand File Compression

Compress Files

Extract Compressed Files

To gain an understanding of the above features, work through the **Driving Lessons** in this **Section**.

For each **Driving Lesson**, read the **Park and Read** instructions, without touching the keyboard, then work through the numbered steps of the **Manoeuvres** on the computer. Complete the **Revision Exercise(s)** at the end of the section to test your knowledge.

Driving Lesson 49 - File Compression

▣ Park and Read

Modern computer applications often involve very large files. Multimedia files in particular, e.g. images, videos and sound, can occupy megabytes of space. This can create problems of storage and more importantly, of transferring such large files. Sending megabytes of data as an e-mail attachment or downloading enormous files from the Internet can be tedious or impractical.

Fortunately programs exist which are able to compress files down to a fraction of their original size so that they can be stored or transmitted much more easily. The files cannot be used in their compressed state, but must be uncompressed (using the same program) before use.

Another feature of compression software is that it can compress several files into a single archive file, which makes handling the compressed files even easier.

For example the **NetMeeting** folder in the *Windows XP* system contains the following assorted files.

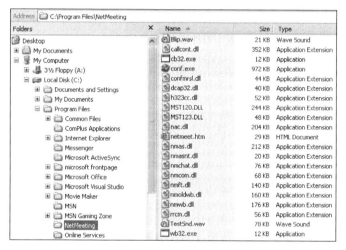

A total of 21 files occupying about 3 MB.

Using *WinZip*, a popular compression program, all these files can be compressed to a single archive file of about 1.2 MB (which would now fit on a floppy disk for example).

This file can be easily transmitted to another user who can then uncompress it and so recreate the original files on their computer. *Windows XP* has the compressing/uncompressing feature built in.

Driving Lesson 50 - Compress Files

 Park and Read

Windows XP contains a basic file compression feature so there is no need to install any additional programs. There are, however, other stand-alone file compression programs which could be used.

Windows creates compressed files in folders with **.zip** extensions. Further files can be added to the **.zip** folder and they will automatically be compressed. The process of compressing files this way is sometimes called **zipping** because of the file extension of the final folder. The compressed files are often called **zipped** files.

If folders are zipped, all content including subfolders will be compressed into the **.zip** folder.

Manoeuvres

1. Open the **My Documents** window.

2. Open **CIA DATA FILES**, then **ECDL**, and finally display the contents of the **2 Managing Files** folder.

3. Click on the **Clothing** file to select it, hold down the **<Ctrl>** key and click on the **Contents** file.

4. With both files selected, right click on either of them and select **Send To**.

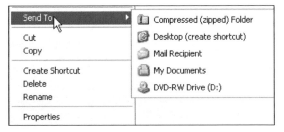

5. Select the **Compressed (zipped) Folder** option.

6. A new folder is created with a **.zip** extension. Rename this folder as **Pack**.

7. Double click on the **Pack.zip** folder to display its contents. It contains compressed copies of the two files.

Driving Lesson 50 - Continued

Name ▲	Type	Packed Size	Has a password	Size	Ratio	Date
Clothing.docx	Microsoft Offi...	9 KB	No	11 KB	25%	02/04/2008 10:31
Contents.docx	Microsoft Offi...	8 KB	No	11 KB	25%	02/04/2008 10:31

> *The file display above may look different as it can be customised. Click and drag column borders to resize them. Click and drag column headers to change the order. Right click a column header to change which columns are displayed or hidden.*

8. More files can be added to the zipped folder at any time. Display the contents of the **2 Managing Files** folder.

9. Use click and drag (or any other method) to copy the **Mailing** file into the **Pack** folder.

10. Display the contents of the **Pack.zip** folder again.

Name ▲	Type	Packed Size	Has a password	Size	Ratio	Date
Clothing.docx	Microsoft Offi...	9 KB	No	11 KB	25%	02/04/2008 10:31
Contents.docx	Microsoft Offi...	8 KB	No	11 KB	25%	02/04/2008 10:31
Mailing.accdb	Microsoft Offi...	13 KB	No	292 KB	96%	02/04/2008 10:47

11. Notice that because the **Mailing** file has been added to a zipped folder, it has been automatically compressed.

12. This zipped folder can be processed like any other, i.e. moved, copied, renamed, deleted. For example it could be sent as an e-mail attachment (size about 29KB) and unzipped by the recipient to obtain the original content (size about 314KB).

13. Close the **Pack.zip** window.

14. Stand-alone compression programs are also available. Starting such a program will display a window like this one for *WinZip*.

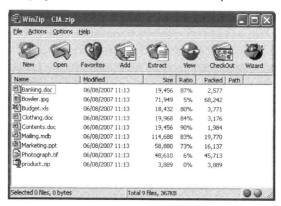

15. Navigate to the appropriate location, select the required folders/files and click **Add** to create a compressed file.

Driving Lesson 51 - Uncompress Files

▣ Park and Read

Before a compressed file can be used, it is advisable to uncompress (extract) it. For files and folders compressed by *Windows XP* this is a very easy process. For example if a zipped *Word* document (**.zip**) is received, it cannot be opened in *Word* until it has been unzipped back to a **.docx** file. This is usually done using the same software that compressed the file. First the archive file is opened, then some or all of the files within can be **extracted** back to their original form. Alternatively some files can be opened directly from the *WinZip* window.

⌫ Manoeuvres

1. Display the contents of the **Pack.zip** folder and click ⬚ Extract all files from the options at the left (make sure **Folders View** is not selected or the button will not be visible).

ℹ️ *This dialog box can also be displayed by right clicking on **Pack.zip** and selecting **Extract All** from the shortcut menu. By default the files will be unpacked into a new folder with the same name as the zipped folder (without the **.zip** extension) and in the same location. The destination folder can be changed either by overtyping the path shown or using the **Browse** button.*

2. Click **Next** then **Next** again, then **Finish**. A new **Pack** folder appears in the **2 Managing Files** folder. It contains uncompressed copies of the three files that were compressed originally.

ℹ️ *To uncompress a file compressed by standalone programs, double click on the compressed file to start the relevant application, then use the **Extract** button.*

3. Close any windows.

Driving Lesson 52 - Revision

This Driving Lesson covers the features introduced in this section. Try not to refer to the previous Driving Lessons while completing it.

> **i** *This exercise requires the use of a File Compression application. If there is not one installed on the computer, the exercise cannot be completed.*

1. Create a new folder in the **My Documents** folder and name it **Compress**.

2. Move the **Mailing** database file from the **2 Managing Files** folder to the **ECDL** folder.

3. Select all the content of the **2 Managing Files** folder and compress them.

4. Rename the zipped folder **Revision.zip** and move it to the **Compress** folder.

5. What is the size of **Revision.zip** and of the original **2 Managing Files** folder?

6. Copy the **Mailing** database from the **ECDL** folder into the **Revision.zip** folder.

7. Extract all the files in **Revision.zip** directly into the **Compress** folder. **Hint:-** Delete the **\Revision** part of the path in the **Extract** dialog box.

8. The **Compress** folder should now contain all the files from **2 Managing Files** folder (including the **Mailing** database), together with the zipped folder **Revision.zip**.

9. Delete the **Compress** folder and all its contents.

10. Move the **Mailing** database file back to the **2 Managing Files** folder from the **ECDL** folder.

11. Close any open windows.

> **i** *Answers to this revision exercise can be found at the end of this guide.*

If you experienced any difficulty completing this exercise, refer back to the Driving Lessons in this section. Then redo the Revision Exercise.

Once you are confident with the features, complete the Record of Achievement Matrix referring to the section at the end of the guide. Only when competent move on to the next Section.

Section 6
Virus Control

By the end of this Section you should be able to:

Understand Viruses

Understand Virus Transmission

Understand Anti-Virus Protection

Use Anti-Virus Protection Applications

To gain an understanding of the above features, work through the **Driving Lessons** in this **Section**.

For each **Driving Lesson**, read the **Park and Read** instructions, without touching the keyboard, then work through the numbered steps of the **Manoeuvres** on the computer. Complete the **Revision Exercise(s)** at the end of the section to test your knowledge.

Driving Lesson 53 - Computer Viruses

🅿 Park and Read

A computer **virus** is a piece of malicious software code introduced to a computer system, with the ability to spread itself to other computers. This should not be confused with the term **bug**, which describes an error or fault in a piece of software code. The extent of the harm caused by viruses varies enormously.

In many cases the contamination remains unnoticed in its host file until a specific event triggers off its action. Viruses can cause many levels of harm to a computer system. The least harmful might cause slightly odd things to happen to a file, for example if a user typed text into a word processed document on an infected computer, certain letters or words might appear on screen in an unexpected text format. Another manifestation of a relatively harmless virus could be the refusal of an application's software to save files to any area other than a specific folder on the HDD, rather than the desired folder on a disk in the floppy drive. The action that a virus carries out when activated is known as the **payload**.

At the other end of the scale, a virus might lie dormant until the built in clock within a PC reaches a certain time on a certain date, or possibly until the computer has been restarted a certain number of times, and then become active. This type of virus is variously known as a **time bomb** or **logic bomb**. It could then destroy the entire file structure as laid down on the HDD and render the HDD completely useless. If this type of virus infected a network, the effect could be catastrophic.

Macro viruses are those that are added to executable files within an application. The most common of these can occur within the **template** files in Microsoft Word and Excel. This is why a user is sometimes given the option of opening such a file with **macros disabled**. If the macro facility can't run, neither can any virus that might be within it!

Driving Lesson 53 - Continued

A **worm** is a self replicating computer program, which uses a computer network to send copies of itself within a system to other computers on the network. It's not a virus, but can open a door for a virus to enter. At best, it simply clogs up the system resources.

A **Trojan** is **malware** and its name comes from the story of the Trojan horse, because it is disguised as a link to a file that a user would be particularly tempted to open, e.g. a game or a graphics file. Once the link is opened, the Trojan gains access to the system.

A common type of virus is one that arrives in an **e-mail attachment**, installs itself within the recipient's *Outlook* or **Contacts** address book and automatically e-mails itself to some or all of the e-mail addresses it finds there. These viruses are particularly effective since the recipient may not realise that the virus has arrived or they have spread the infection onwards. The new victims are less likely to be suspicious of attachments e-mailed to them by a known contact.

Viruses can only become active within a system if they are introduced to the system from outside and then subsequently activated.

It therefore follows that the only pathways available to viruses are via **input devices** such as **floppy disks**, **memory sticks**, **CDs** or **DVDs** or the **Internet**. If genuine application software from reputable sources only is installed on a PC, in theory there should be no danger. If, however, disks containing applications or files are borrowed/acquired from dubious or unknown sources, the chance of them containing viruses is much greater. As indicated above, e-mails received with file attachments are now a prime source of viruses and should be treated with particular caution, as should any files downloaded from the **World Wide Web** that have a **.exe** extension. This extension identifies **executable** files, i.e. files that are actual programs that will open up and run. If the file contains a virus, the virus will run with the program!

Driving Lesson 54 - Anti-Virus Protection

▣ Park and Read

There are two approaches to combat the increasing threat of computer viruses. Firstly modern operating systems such as *Windows XP* are designed to include as many security features as possible, from built in firewall features to user access settings which always prompt for confirmation before executing any functions which could be even potentially hazardous.

In addition to sophisticated operating systems, it is highly recommended to employ a reliable virus protection application. There are many versions of virus protection software available. Basically these operate in two modes.

Firstly, they can **scan** a computer system for existing viruses. These scans can be started manually or can be put on a schedule so that they run at certain times. All or part of the system can be scanned. Most protection applications also offer the option of removing viruses that are found and reversing their effects where possible. This process is known as **disinfecting**.

Secondly, they can run continuously to **shield** a system from any incoming viruses. Possible sources of viruses such as floppy disks and network connections are automatically checked and reported on if necessary. Some applications extend this cover in certain circumstances by checking e-mail even before it has been processed by the computer.

Unfortunately all virus protection programs currently have an inherent problem. They work by scanning the code in a system and comparing it to a list of all known viruses. If a match is found, a virus has been detected. It follows then that the only viruses a protection system can detect are ones it already knows about. When a new virus first appears, the protection software company must identify it and add it to their list of known viruses. The user must then obtain a copy of this new list to update their system before they are protected against the new virus. So it is not enough to install and run virus protection software, it must be continuously updated.

Most protection applications can be updated by downloading the current virus list (or the new additions to it) via the Internet on a regular basis. Some systems can even transmit new additions to virus lists automatically as they become available. It is worth remembering however that at present, no protection system will detect viruses that have appeared since the virus list was last updated.

Driving Lesson 54 - Continued

Anti-virus measures

Taking certain basic safety precautions will reduce the chances of infection:

- Install reliable **anti-virus software** and **update** it regularly.
- Use the software to carry out **regular scans** of the **entire system**.
- Use the software to scan **any removable disk** that is placed in a drive on the system **before installing or opening any files** from it.
- Be conscious about the **source** of any software you use!
- **Save any files downloaded from the Internet**, either to a floppy disk or to the HDD and **scan them with anti-virus software before opening** them.
- Be particularly suspicious of **any e-mail messages containing attachments** from an unknown source.
- Even be suspicious of **any e-mail messages** from an unknown source.
- **Do not open anything suspicious, virus-scan everything!**

Anti-spam Software

Spam mails are a used by many companies as a way of advertising, as it is relatively easy to do. We all get e-mails about medicines, car insurance, etc. However, apart from being annoying, spam mails can be a way of introducing viruses to your computer. Anti-spam software is an effective way of filtering these unwanted messages and is often included with your anti-virus software.

Firewall

Every computer should have an operational **firewall**. A firewall is effectively a filter that determines what type of traffic is allowed to pass out of the system to the Internet, and into the system from the Internet.

Driving Lesson 55 - Anti-Virus Protection Applications

▣ Park and Read

There are many versions of virus protection software available from a range of suppliers. As an example, this Driving Lesson will look at one: *Norton Internet Security* available from *Symantec*.

⌒ Manoeuvres

1. Locate the **Virus Protection** application on the computer. It could have

    been installed as a desktop icon, 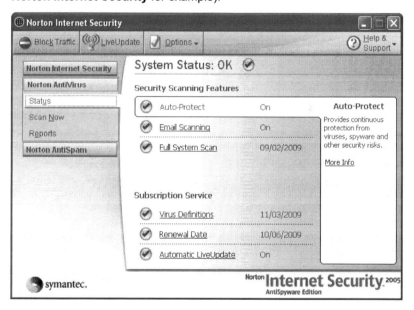 or as a button on the **Taskbar**, or it may be found in the **Start** menu (by clicking **Start | All Programs | Norton Internet Security** for example).

2. Select the **Scan Now** tab to define where to search and click **Scan my computer**.

Driving Lesson 55 - Continued

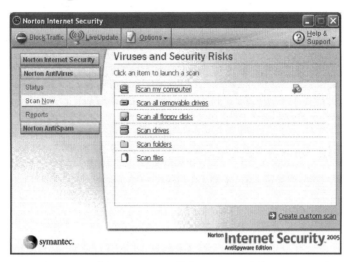

3.   The selected areas of the system will be scanned for known viruses. If one is found you will be asked what action to take.

4.   When the scan is finished, close down any **Norton Internet Security** windows that may be open.

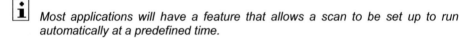

Most applications will have a feature that allows a scan to be set up to run automatically at a predefined time.

5.   Most applications allow individual files to be scanned. Right click on a file in any file display window, e.g. **My Computer**, and select **Scan with...** from the shortcut menu. Note that in some applications this option is only available for certain file types.

Driving Lesson 56 - Revision

This Driving Lesson covers the features introduced in this section. Try not to refer to the previous Driving Lessons while completing it.

Indicate whether each of the statements 1 to 10 is **True** or **False**?

1. Viruses do not cause any real damage.

2. Viruses only affect business computers.

3. A virus can be transmitted via a document on a floppy disk.

4. A virus can be transmitted between computers on a network.

5. A virus can be transmitted via an e-mail.

6. If your computer is working OK then you do not have a virus.

7. The only way to remove a virus is to reformat the entire hard disk.

8. Virus protection software can scan a removable storage device such as a floppy disk or memory stick.

9. Once you install and run virus protection software you will never get another virus.

10. Virus protection can be set to automatically check incoming data.

11. Bill Sticker, the Office Manager at CIA World has said that he will not be installing any Virus Protection software on the Company's computers because '**it will cost too much money**'. From what you know about viruses, write a short report listing some of the possible costs that might be incurred if a virus establishes itself on the computer system in a busy office.

 *Answers to this revision exercise can be found at the end of this guide.*

If you experienced any difficulty completing the Revision, refer back to the Driving Lessons in this section. Then redo the Revision.

Once you are confident with the features, complete the Record of Achievement Matrix referring to the section at the end of the guide. Only when competent move on to the next Section.

Section 7
Control Panel

By the end of this Section you should be able to:

Change Date and Time

Control the Background

Choose a Screen Saver

Select Settings and Effects

Control Sound and Multimedia

To gain an understanding of the above features, work through the **Driving Lessons** in this **Section**.

For each **Driving Lesson**, read the **Park and Read** instructions, without touching the keyboard, then work through the numbered steps of the **Manoeuvres** on the computer. Complete the **Revision Exercise(s)** at the end of the section to test your knowledge.

Driving Lesson 57 - Control Panel

▣ Park and Read

The **Control Panel** contains tools that control how the *Windows* environment looks and performs. Any changes made are permanent until changed again. The changes made will still be in effect after closing down and restarting *Windows*.

The default view of the **Control Panel** is the **Category View**, where similar functions are grouped together under category headings.

Categories include:

 To change **Desktop** appearance, apply a theme or screen saver, customise the **Start** menu and **Taskbar**

 To create or view Internet and network connections

 To add or remove programs or *Windows* components

 To change sound schemes, configure settings for speakers and recording

 For maintenance and optimisation of the hard disk drive

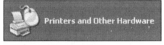 To change settings for printers, keyboard, mouse and other hardware

 To change user accounts, passwords and pictures

 To change date, time, time zone, language and number display

 To adjust settings for hearing, vision and mobility.

 To view current security status and adjust settings.

Driving Lesson 57 - Continued

Manoeuvres

1. Click the **Start** button on the **Taskbar**.

2. Select **Control Panel**. The **Control Panel** window appears.

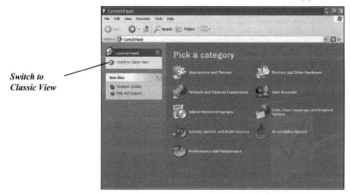

Switch to Classic View

3. Click on **Switch to Classic View** to display the alternative view of the **Control Panel**, more familiar to users of earlier versions of *Windows*.

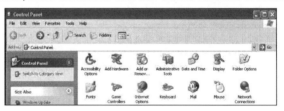

4. Double click the **Regional and Language Options** icon. Select the **Regional Options** tab. Look at the settings here, which control properties such as date, number and currency format. The default setting for the UK is **English (United Kingdom).**

5. Select the **Languages** tab and click the **Details** button under **Text services and input languages**. Look at the settings here, which control the **Input Language** and **Keyboard** settings for the system. The default setting for the UK is **English (United Kingdom) - United Kingdom** for the language and keyboard respectively. Take care if changing settings here, the keyboard may no longer respond as expected.

6. To add a keyboard language, click **Add** and select from the **Input Language** drop down list. Click **OK** to add another keyboard language otherwise click **Cancel**.

7. Close all **Regional and Language Options** boxes.

8. In the **Control Panel** window, click **Switch to Category View** to display the default view and leave the window open.

Driving Lesson 58 - Date and Time

▣ Park and Read

The computer has a built in clock and calendar. On occasion, the time or date may need to be changed. Modern computers can be set to adjust automatically for the clocks going forward or back. Take care if planning to alter the date or time on a networked computer as the system may need to have all components synchronised.

☞ Manoeuvres

1.   From the **Control Panel**, double click on the **Date, Time, Language and Regional Options** category then click [Date and Time]. This opens the **Date and Time Properties** dialog box.

2.   Check that the date and time are correct. Make any necessary changes using the appropriate boxes.

3.   Select the **Time Zone** tab and make sure that the computer is using the correct time zone.

ℹ️   *If the option to **Automatically adjust clock for daylight saving changes** is checked, the clock will go forward or back as necessary.*

4.   Click **Cancel** to close the dialog box without keeping any of the changes or click **OK** to accept the changes.

5.   To display the **Date and Time Properties** dialog box using an alternative method, double click on the **Time** on the **Taskbar**.

6.   Click the **Cancel** button or the **Close** button to close the dialog box, then click on the **Toolbar** to return to the **Control Panel** and leave it open.

Driving Lesson 59 - Display Options

▣ Park and Read

The *Windows* display can be personalised to suit the user. All the colours, patterns, fonts, etc., used on screen can be changed in a number of ways.

⌒ Manoeuvres

1. From the **Control Panel**, select the **Appearance and Themes** category and then click the **Display** icon to open the **Display Properties** dialog box.

i *Alternatively, to open the dialog box, right click on any empty area of the **Desktop** and select **Properties** from the shortcut menu.*

i *The available tabs within **Display Properties** may differ according to the version of the software installed.*

2. From the **Desktop** tab, various **Background** pictures and **Position** settings can be combined to produce the screen backgrounds required.

3. Select each of the tabs at the top of the dialog box in turn and examine the options.

4. Leave the **Display Properties** box open for the next Driving Lesson.

Driving Lesson 60 - Screen Saver

▣ Park and Read

A **screen saver** is a moving pattern or message that appears on the screen when the computer hasn't been used for a set period of time. Originally this was to save the screen from having the same picture burned into it. A **password** can also be set to ensure that the screen saver will continue until the password is entered.

⟨ͤ Manoeuvres

1. Select the **Screen Saver** tab from the **Display Properties** dialog box, if not already selected.

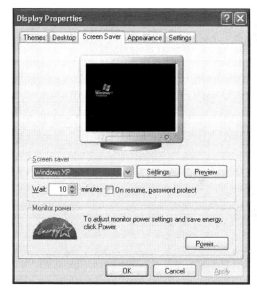

2. Click on the drop down **Screen Saver** list and select each available screen saver in turn, noticing the effect in the sample screen. Select **Settings** for each one to see the options that can be varied.

3. Select **Preview** for a few, to see the effect on the screen (as soon as the mouse is moved the **Preview** will end).

4. Select a **Wait** time. This is the amount of time the computer has to be idle before it activates the screen saver.

5. Click **Apply** to apply the current settings.

6. Leave the dialog box open for the next Driving Lesson.

Driving Lesson 61 - Settings and Effects

⊞ Park and Read

The **Settings** tab gives choices on the number of colours used on the screen and the resolution (quality) of the graphics. The **Appearance** tab allows icons to be changed, both in size and appearance.

⟲ Manoeuvres

1. Select the **Settings** tab of the **Display Properties** dialog box.

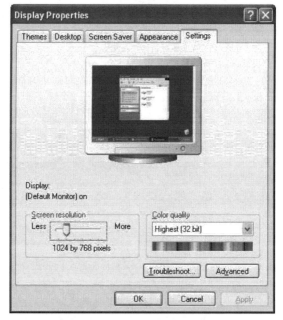

2. From here it is possible to change the **Color quality**, the number of colours used by the display, and **Screen resolution**, which defines the pixel resolution of the display (1024 by 768 pixels is the most common but the setting is dependent on the installed video card and the user's eyesight). Do **not** change anything. Look at all of the available settings.

3. Select the **Appearance** tab and click the **Effects** button.

4. Click on **Use large icons** and click **OK**. Click **Apply**. The icons on the desktop will now be large.

5. Click **Effects**, uncheck **Use large icons**, click **OK** then click **Apply** again to return them to their original size.

6. Click **Cancel** to close the **Display Properties** dialog box.

Driving Lesson 62 - Sound

🅿 Park and Read

Sounds can be assigned to various **events** in *Windows* by using the **Sounds and Multimedia Properties** dialog box. A list of events is shown, those with sounds attached are indicated by a speaker icon.

🏁 Manoeuvres

1. In the **Control Panel** window double click **Sounds and Audio Devices**. If **Category View** is active open the **Sounds, Speech and Audio Devices** category first.

2. Click the **Sounds** tab.

3. Select any of the **Program Events** with a sound attached, (🔊), and click the **Play** button, ▶, to hear the sound.

ℹ️ *The speakers need to be attached, switched on and the volume controls set.*

4. Click the **Volume** tab of the dialog box. The overall sound volume level is controlled by the **Device volume** slider. Move the slider and note the difference when playing sounds.

5. Click the **Audio** tab to see controls for individual audio processes. Note that each process has its own **Volume** slider.

6. Click the **Volume** tab and make sure **Place volume icon in the taskbar** is checked. Click **OK**. A volume control icon, 🔊, will appear at the right of the **Taskbar**.

ℹ️ *It may be necessary to click* ◀ *on the Taskbar to reveal the icons.*

7. Click on the volume control icon on the **Taskbar** to display a simplified **Volume** slider.

8. Click and drag the slider to vary the sound level then click on a blank area of **Desktop** to remove it.

9. Close the **Control Panel**.

Driving Lesson 63 - Revision

This Driving Lesson covers the features introduced in this section. Try not to refer to the previous Driving Lessons while completing it.

1. Check what day your birthday will fall on next year using the **Date/Time Properties**.

2. Restore the correct settings.

3. Change the **Desktop Background** to **Soap Bubbles, Stretch**.

4. Change the **Screen Saver** to **Mystify**, to come on after **2 minutes**.

5. Change the **Color Scheme** to **Silver**.

6. Return the display to its original settings by selecting **None** for **Background** and **Screen Saver** and **Default** for the **Color Scheme**.

7. Make sure you have a speaker icon on the **Taskbar**.

8. Double click the speaker icon to display a **Volume Control** dialog box.

9. Single click the speaker icon display the volume slider.

10. Drag the slider up and down. What happens to the **Volume Control** settings?

11. Close the **Volume Control** dialog box.

12. Close the **Control Panel**.

13. Exit *Windows*.

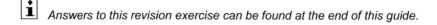 *Answers to this revision exercise can be found at the end of this guide.*

If you experienced any difficulty completing this exercise, refer back to the Driving Lessons in this section. Then redo the Revision Exercise.

Once you are confident with the features, complete the Record of Achievement Matrix referring to the section at the end of the guide. Only when competent move on to the next Section.

Section 8
Systems Maintenance

By the end of this Section you should be able to:

Understand the importance of systems maintenance

Carry out routine maintenance

Know when specialists should carry out maintenance

Identify IT problems and know how to resolve them

To gain an understanding of the above features, work through the **Driving Lessons** in this **Section**.

For each **Driving Lesson**, read the **Park and Read** instructions, without touching the keyboard, then work through the numbered steps of the **Manoeuvres** on the computer. Complete the **Revision Exercise(s)** at the end of the section to test your knowledge.

Driving Lesson 64 - Maintaining Systems

▣ Park and Read

Routine maintenance keeps your computer healthy. *Windows* has various tools that help to keep your PC running at its top performance. The **Check Disk** tool scans the hard drive for damage, both physical and logical. The **Disk Defragmenter** locates fragmented files and folders on local drives and puts the pieces together in one place. **Disk Cleanup** lets you get rid of unnecessary files and makes the most of the hard disk space. This tool lets you decide which unwanted files to remove.

As time goes by and you fill your computer's hard disk with music, videos and files, you may notice it becomes noticeably slower. This is often the reason why people "upgrade" their computer's hardware, by adding more memory or hard disk space. Upgrading hardware, as well as fixing hardware failures such as malfunctioning hard disks and power supplies, is considered non-routine maintenance and an experienced specialist technician should be consulted.

Unwanted programs can be deleted via the **Control Panel**, but additionally you should check **My Documents** for unwanted files and remove them, probably on a weekly basis, but at least regularly.

⌒ Manoeuvres

1. To locate the **Check Disk** tool, select **Start | All Programs | Accessories | System Tools | Disk Cleanup**.

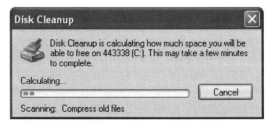

2. This tool calculates how much space can be freed and then displays the results. Decide which files you want to remove by checking the appropriate boxes.

Driving Lesson 64 - Continued

3.   Click **OK** to start the process.

4.   To start the defragmenter, select **Start | All Programs | Accessories | System Tools | Disk Defragmenter**.

5.   Select the drive to be defragmented, and to see how this will be done, click **Analyze**.

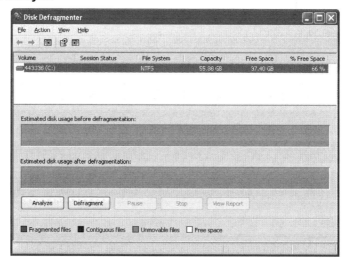

Driving Lesson 64 - Continued

6.   If you want to go ahead, click **Defragment**. Make sure though, that no other programs are running and that any screen saver is turned off. Defragmentation takes a long time, so it might be best to perform this task when you have something else to do, not requiring the use of your computer.

7.   To check the hard disk for errors, open **My Computer** and right click on the hard disk icon, then select **Properties**. From the **Tools** tab, click **Check Now**.

8.   Select options carefully and click **Start**. Follow the on-screen instructions, closing all windows when finished.

9.   Unwanted programs should only be deleted if you are <u>absolutely certain</u> they are no longer required. To do this, open the **Control Panel** and double click **Add or Remove Programs**. Currently installed programs are displayed. Select the program to be removed and click **Remove**.

Driving Lesson 65 - Cleaning Hardware

▣ Park and Read

It's important to routinely clean your computer hardware to maintain functionality and appearance. General cleaning instructions are given below, but you may need to refer to the manufacturer's documentation; remember to always dispose of cleaning materials safely.

Screen

Clean with the appropriate wipes - do not press hard on TFT screens. For laptop screens, a wipe with a damp (not wet) cloth is enough. Be careful not to get any liquid into the computer parts.

Keyboard

Unplug the keyboard and turn it upside down. Shake to remove crumbs, dust, etc. Spray between the keys with compressed air. Clean the keys with a mild cleaning agent or rubbing alcohol - don't use too much liquid. Let the keyboard dry and then plug it in.

Mouse

Unplug the mouse, dampen a paper towel with a mild cleaning agent and wipe the top and bottom. This is enough for an optical mouse. If the mouse has a ball, remove the cover on the underneath and remove fluff/dust from the rollers inside. Clean the wheels with cleaning agent; take the dust/fluff off the ball and run it under water. Dry thoroughly and replace in the mouse.

Case

Turn the computer off and unplug it. Outside: dampen a paper towel with a mild cleaning agent and wipe the case down - don't use too much liquid. Inside: remove the casing. Use compressed air to clean dust out of the vents and fan in the back. Use short bursts of air, blowing in one direction, to clean circuit boards, drives, etc. Replace the case.

CD/DVD Drive

Open the drive and blow compressed air into it. To prevent introducing dust into the drive, make sure disks are clean before inserting them.

Driving Lesson 66 - Dealing with Problems

▣ Park and Read

In the course of using a computer you will come across various error messages in dialog boxes, e.g. a program has stopped responding, storage facilities are full, there's a paper jam in the printer, you've lost a network connection, or your computer has been threatened by a virus. Error messages are designed to grab your attention, explain what the problem is and to suggest possible solutions.

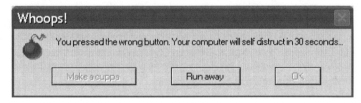

There are various courses of action you can take to deal with these problems; *Windows* generally gives some guidance in the message boxes. For example, if a program has stopped responding there is an option to **End Now** - *Windows* will try to recover any work in programs such as *Word* or *Excel*. If you get a message that storage is full when you're saving work, try to get rid of any unwanted data (see Driving Lesson 64 on **Maintaining Systems**) and then try saving again - you could always save temporarily on to a memory stick while trying to resolve this problem. If you see an error message regarding a paper jam, try to clear the jam to remove the message (see Driving Lesson 36 on **Printer Maintenance**). Should a lost network connection message appear, check any physical connections, i.e. wires; if it's a wireless connection, make sure the wireless box is switched on and working correctly. Any messages regarding virus threats will normally originate from your anti-virus software - sometimes it is simply informing you that an attempt to access your computer has been blocked. Carefully read any options given before taking any action.

If you don't know what action to take to deal with a problem, you must ask someone who may be able to help. There are various sources of help available to you: help menus included in the program; manufacturer's guidelines; experienced colleagues.

In some situations, however, you may need to get expert advice; perhaps from your IT administrator, a technician, or a help line. You will need to know how to deal with the advice you are given and be prepared to provide them with information. For example, they will need to know exactly what error message has appeared, with a reference number if one is shown. You may need to tell them what type of computer you are using and which operating system. If you call a help line, they may talk you through the process to resolve the problem. Follow their advice to the letter and if you don't understand, ask them to repeat the instructions. If you feel you don't have the skills to do what you are advised, then say so and find someone who can take over and help you work through the instructions.

Driving Lesson 67 - Revision

This Driving Lesson covers the features introduced in this section. Try not to refer to the previous Driving Lessons while completing it.

1.   Why should you perform routine maintenance?

2.   Name 2 ways to get rid of unwanted files.

3.   How would you clean an optical mouse?

4.   List some sources of help when problems are encountered.

i   *Answers to this revision exercise can be found at the end of this guide.*

If you experienced any difficulty completing this exercise, refer back to the Driving Lessons in this section. Then redo the Revision Exercise.

Once you are confident with the features, complete the Record of Achievement Matrix referring to the section at the end of the guide. Only when competent move on to the next Section.

Section 9
Health & Safety
Environment

By the end of this Section you should be able to:

Identify Health & Safety Issues

Understand how to help protect the Environment

To gain an understanding of the above features, work through the **Driving Lessons** in this **Section**.

For each **Driving Lesson**, read the **Park and Read** instructions, without touching the keyboard, then work through the numbered steps of the **Manoeuvres** on the computer. Complete the **Revision Exercise(s)** at the end of the section to test your knowledge.

Driving Lesson 68 - Health and Safety

▣ Park and Read

Ergonomics

The term **ergonomics** refers to the relationship between workers and their working environment. The following aspects of the working environment should be taken into account when assessing whether or not a working environment is suitable for computer operation and whether or not it conforms to legislation:

- ◆ Provision of adequate lighting

- ◆ Provision of adequate ventilation

- ◆ VDUs appropriately positioned with screens free from flicker and interference and images free from glare

- ◆ Provision of monitor filters/anti-glare screens if required

- ◆ Suitability and adjustability of chair to provide the prescribed posture for the user, i.e. feet on the floor and a comfortable height in relation to the desk

- ◆ Provision of a mouse mat or suitable equivalent surface

- ◆ Suitably positioned keyboard, not too far away from the user

- ◆ Provision for frequent breaks away from the computer (10mins after every 50mins work).

It is an employer's responsibility to ensure that appropriate provisions are made available, but the employee has a responsibility to ensure that he/she makes use of them and goes about their job in an appropriate manner. They should make sure they take regular breaks, but also stretch their arms and legs from time to time while at the desk. They should also make time to relax their eyes when working with the computer. A workplace that has swivel chairs with adjustable positions, stable, roomy desks, etc. will provide a working environment that is comfortable and safe. If a computer, desk and chair are correctly positioned, they will help the user to maintain a good posture. Furniture and equipment needs to be suitably positioned, appropriate to the type of work for which it is intended and to conform to the relevant Health and Safety at Work (HASAW) legislation.

Lighting must be adequate to work comfortably, particularly if it is necessary to read documents whilst working. Positioning of light must be arranged so as not to cause glare reflection on the screen or distraction directly behind it. Artificial lighting can cause its own problems, and efforts should be made to provide natural light where possible, or good quality artificial light which attempts to reproduce natural light characteristics.

Driving Lesson 68 - Continued

Health Issues

Injuries common in an IT environment are:

- Aches and pains (especially to the **back**) due to bad posture when seated for long periods

- Repetitive strain injury (**RSI**) caused by poor ergonomics combined with repeated movements of the same joints, e.g. **wrist**, over a long period of time

- **Eye strain** which can be caused by **glare** or flickering from a VDU and by not taking regular visual breaks (10 minutes every hour is recommended) away from the screen

- Injuries due to tripping over trailing wires or other obstructions.

Precautions

In any work environment you must recognise that there are risks associated with using IT. Make sure:

- you take care when handling equipment, especially when moving or carrying heavy items

- the hardware and electrical items you use have been safety checked

- there are no trailing or **insecure power leads** or other cables

- there are no worn or frayed power leads

- there are no **overloaded power points**.

You need to know the relevant guidelines and procedures for the safe and secure use of IT in your organisation and, in any work environment, your employer must display the health and safety policy in a prominent place. Make sure you know where the policy is in your place of work. You can find up to date information on health and safety laws and guidelines that specifically affect the use of IT on the web site of the Health and Safety Executive **www.hse.gov.uk**. The relevant law is the **Health and Safety (Display Screen Equipment) Regulations 1992**.

The Environment

IT equipment and consumables must be disposed of correctly and safely. Some components such as monitors, batteries, wiring and toner cartridges contain chemicals which are harmful to the environment. Broken computers, monitors, etc. cannot just be disposed of with normal waste; they must be taken to a special facility for safe dismantling/recycling. Cleaning materials must also be disposed of responsibly.

Driving Lesson 68 - Continued

It is also desirable that certain steps be taken in an IT workplace to minimise the effect of working practices on the environment.

- ♦ Where possible **recycle waste paper**

- ♦ Where possible **recycle ink/toner cartridges** from printers and copiers

- ♦ Where possible use energy efficient monitors with **low power** options

- ♦ Use PC settings that enable "sleep" (or **standby**) mode for HDDs and monitors when the devices are inactive

- ♦ Where possible save documents in an electronic format within the computer system rather than printing out hard copies.

Manoeuvres

1. How would you ensure that your **working environment** was safe?

2. As an employee, what are your responsibilities towards your own **safety** in the workplace?

3. What precautions could you take to minimise the effect of your work on the environment?

Driving Lesson 69 - Revision

This Driving Lesson covers the features introduced in this section. Try not to refer to the preceding Driving Lessons while completing it.

1.　What is meant by **HASAW**?

2.　Describe a **good working environment** relevant to PC use.

3.　What is **RSI**?

4.　Describe some **Health and Safety precautions** which should be taken when working with computers.

5.　What **common injuries** might occur in such an environment?

6.　What do you understand by the term **ergonomics**?

7.　What two things can you do to save paper?

If you experienced any difficulty completing this exercise, refer back to the Driving Lessons in this section. Then redo the Revision Exercise.

Once you are confident with the features, complete the Record of Achievement Matrix referring to the section at the end of the guide. Only when competent move on to the next Section.

Section 10
Security

By the end of this Section you should be able to:

Understand the need for Backing up Data

Know about Privacy Issues

Understand the Information Security Issues

Understand Safe and Proper Practice

Understand Copyright Legislation

Know about the Data Protection Act

To gain an understanding of the above features, work through the **Driving Lessons** in this **Section**.

For each **Driving Lesson**, read the **Park and Read** instructions, without touching the keyboard, then work through the numbered steps of the **Manoeuvres** on the computer. Complete the **Revision Exercise(s)** at the end of the section to test your knowledge.

Driving Lesson 70 - Security Issues

P Park and Read

Backing Up

In an earlier section, the fact that certain parts of a PC's memory are only temporary was discussed. It is, therefore, good practice to save your work to permanent storage (HDD or file server) after regular, short periods. This ensures that if a power cut occurs, only the data produced since the last save is lost. Certain software applications perform this task automatically.

Apart from protecting data against loss due to power failure, an organisation needs to consider the possibility of total file loss due to: a serious hardware fault, physical damage to the computer (possibly as a result of fire), infection by computer virus, theft or other malicious action.

The loss of vital files may be inconvenient to an individual using a home PC for hobby purposes, but to a business user, large or small, the loss could well be catastrophic. It is, therefore, essential for strategies to be available that enable regular, complete copies to be made of all files which are identified as being critical to an organisation. This is known as **backing up** files and may be carried out hourly, daily, weekly or in any combination thereof. Regular backing up ensures that even in the event of a total loss of data, an organisation has an almost current, duplicate set of its most important files, which it can rely upon to maintain business continuity.

Storage containing the backed up material is known as **backing store** and should be treated as a very valuable commodity. The fundamental reason for backing up files is to ensure that they cannot be lost, or completely destroyed, while saved on the hard drive of the PC or the file server. It is, therefore, not totally secure to keep the backing store in the same room, or even building, as the source material because of the risk of fire.

For absolute security, the backing store should be removed from the working environment (off site) and more than one set of backing store media should be used in rotation. All backup media should be kept in a storage environment, which is theft-proof, fireproof and waterproof.

Driving Lesson 70 - Continued

For an individual home PC user, such sophisticated techniques are unnecessary; however some backing up should be carried out. Always try to bear in mind how much time and effort would be lost if your PC either switched itself off or blew up! If the former happened, you would lose all unsaved work, if the latter, you would lose all work saved onto your HDD as well as all application software installed on your machine. It is good practice to keep all the original media on which application software is supplied, i.e. program CDs in a safe place.

It is highly likely that at some point, for whatever reason, you will need to re-install application software. You should also make a point of backing up all files that you have created yourself and saved to disk.

Privacy Issues

If there is any need to consider the content of certain files as being sensitive or confidential, the use of password protection should be used to prevent unauthorised persons accessing, viewing or editing the data. A **password** typically acts as a user's **personal** entry code to their own PC, software or files and would usually be chosen by the user and never divulged to anyone. A perfect password will consist of a combination of letters and numbers and be of an adequate length, e.g. 8 characters, not just 3. Don't use something too simple like your name, date of birth or your dog's name. You should <u>never</u> share a password, or for that matter a PIN number, with another person. **Passwords** should be changed regularly, to prevent the possibility of misuse by unauthorised individuals.

As well as **password** protection, most organisations or systems would require the use of a **user ID** (otherwise referred to as a **user-name** or **log-in name**.) This is another level of access code that provides evidence of a user's entitlement to access certain areas of a network or system. A **user ID** would typically be assigned to users by the relevant organisation, i.e. the owner / administrator of the system or network in question. A number of users might be given the same **user** ID. This would identify to the system the fact that the user could legitimately claim access to the network, also, it would identify the level of access to which the user was entitled. The **password** would also be necessary to identify the individual user, and provide evidence of their entitlement to access their own files, within an area of the network designated as "theirs". *See information on **Authentication**, **Identification** and **Authorisation** later in this Driving Lesson.*

Driving Lesson 70 - Continued

It is feasible therefore, <u>if full use is made of password protection facilities</u>, for the following security measures to be in place when a user starts up a networked PC:

- ◆ A **password** must be typed in to gain access to the PC.

- ◆ A **user ID** must be typed in to gain access to the network or system.

- ◆ A **password** must be entered to gain access to shared directory space on the network server.

- ◆ A **password** must be typed in to gain access to a file saved in that directory space.

- ◆ A **password** must be typed in to gain authority to amend the file content by saving changes.

The different levels of access given by different **user ID**s are known as **access rights**. It is important that organisations have security policies in place with regard to **access rights**, in order that only appropriate personnel have access to the system and only appropriate personnel have access to sensitive parts of the system. These security precautions should be taken on top of normal, sensible physical security measures such as burglar alarms, locks and keys, etc.

There are three processes that are activated when a user logs on to a computer system: **Authentication**, **Identification** and **Authorisation**. Authentication is simply the process to find out if someone is who they are saying they are, i.e. on computer networks authentication is carried out by checking log on user passwords. The process of identification connects the information you have given in your user name and password and checks that it matches the details held for you. Once you've been authenticated and identified, then the authorisation process checks if you have the required permissions to access the content. This is a bit like the computer saying, "I know who you are, now I'm checking what you're allowed to do."

Information Security

This term is used to describe methods for ensuring that data stored on a computer system is protected against being compromised, or against unauthorised access. It is important that any organisation should have an **active** policy to ensure that security is not compromised, rather than waiting to deal with any breach once it has happened.

Driving Lesson 70 - Continued

An **information security policy** should document such issues as:

- The details of a **user ID/password** policy as described above
- The **personnel responsible** for each level of security
- **Anti-virus** measures
- Penalties for **breaching security policy**
- Procedures for **reporting security incidents**
- Procedures for educating staff about their **responsibilities** regarding **information security**

As part of overall security consciousness, individuals should be aware of the sensitive nature of information stored in portable appliances such as **laptops**, **PDAs** and **mobile phones**. If such a device was lost or **stolen**, not only could **confidential files** fall into the wrong hands but personal information (**addresses**, **phone numbers** etc.) could be misused by the finder and **contact details** could be lost to the company. All such devices should be kept safe at all times and password protection should be applied wherever available, also, as much of the material as possible should be included in any **backup** regime.

 Manoeuvres

1. Why is it good practice to **regularly save** to permanent storage?

2. Why should at least one set of **backing store** media be kept **off site**?

3. Describe the possible levels of **password protection** that may be applied to networked files.

Driving Lesson 71 - Safe and Proper Practice

▣ Park and Read

When using ICT based communication you need to know how to keep personal information safe but, equally, you need to respect the privacy and data of other people.

Personal Data

You can protect your data by using a user name and password and, on a more physical level, you can lock your computer and hardware with a security cable. When using the Internet, you must make sure you protect personal information. When making purchases on the Internet it will usually be necessary to supply financial data (usually credit or debit card details) to the seller. This process involves some risk (although probably no more than supplying the same details over the telephone) and so there are protection methods available to make the process safer. Making online financial transactions with a bank or insurance company for example carry the same level of risk.

Many web sites cannot be accessed without a user name and password; these are called protected sites. Sometimes you have to pay a fee up front before you can access a web site, which can then be done by entering the user name and password allocated to you. You will usually need a user name and password to shop online at supermarkets such as Sainsbury's or Tesco, and to use online financial services. Most sites that involve supplying sensitive financial data, e.g. shopping and banking sites, will be set up as secure sites. This means that all transferred information will be automatically encrypted (scrambled).

These web pages can be identified by https at the start of the URL, and a small padlock symbol, 🔒, on the Status Bar. Always ensure that you are using a secure site before supplying any financial or other sensitive information. Take as much care with your personal details on the Internet as you would in other areas of your life. Do not send financial details unless you are sure of the site and secure access is in force. Only e-mail such information if you are very sure you know where it is going. Always think before giving out details such as name, address and telephone number. This is particularly true in social situations such as e-mail correspondence and chat room activities. It is relatively easy to ignore someone electronically by deleting their e-mails or staying away from a chat room, but not so easy if they have your real name, address and telephone number.

Driving Lesson 71 - Continued

Respect for Others

It's very important to respect other ICT users and indeed their data. Plagiarism, the practice of copying the work of someone else and passing it off as your own, is a growing problem because of the sheer amount of information available on the Internet. It's very easy to copy and paste an essay or some other document - you must not do this. Always acknowledge your sources and be aware of copyright issues. This also applies to misuse of images - you must not use any images in your own work that are subject to copyright.

You must handle confidential information responsibly - make sure it is protected and dealt with in an appropriate manner. For example, don't leave a confidential document open on your computer while you go for a coffee break, and don't leave a CD containing personal names and addresses on the bus!

Be careful about the type of language you use. Although e-mail is often considered a less formal means of communication than other methods you must still make sure your language in not offensive or inappropriate. Before using e-mail, familiarise yourself with the rules of netiquette - network etiquette. Always use accurate and brief subjects in the appropriate field on a message. Keep your messages brief and relevant rather than rambling. Make sure your outgoing messages are spelled correctly and don't write in capitals - it's considered the same as shouting.

When forwarding or addressing messages to several recipients, be discriminating in your use of copy lists. If you use the **Cc** feature, all recipients will be able to see other recipients' e-mail address. Sometimes the **Bcc** feature may be more appropriate, where addresses are kept hidden.

Check the Internet use and e-mail policies in your organisation and make sure you abide by them.

Driving Lesson 72 - Copyright

P Park and Read

Software copyright legislation

Copyright protects creative or artistic works. Software copyright legislation exists to give the authors/developers of software the same legal protection as the authors of published, written and musical works already enjoy. The software legislation is, if anything, more restrictive in practice than traditional copyright laws. If an individual purchases a book or music CD, copyright law prohibits them from copying that material in any way, without the express permission of the author or publisher. They are, however, able to lend their copy of the book or CD to a third party.

Software copyright operates in such a way that an individual who buys a computer program, be it a game, a piece of application software or an operating system, does not actually purchase that item but purchases the right to use it within a specific set of criteria. It is a **single user licence** that has been purchased, allowing the user to install one copy of the software on a single computer on which the program will be run, together with the right to create one backup copy of the software (unless specifically excluded). The licence details accompanying the software will also set out exactly what the user is permitted to do with it without contravening copyright laws.

Due to the widespread use of laptops and other portable PCs, some software licences allow the software to be installed on two machines as long as they are not both used simultaneously. This recognises that more and more users have a desktop PC in their office, as well as a laptop that they carry around, or a desktop machine at home. These users will need to run the same software on both machines and as (in theory) they cannot use two machines at the same time, they are not forced to buy two expensive copies of the same software.

However, unlike a book or an audio CD, a piece of software cannot be loaned to a third party, since that would presumably mean that an unlawful installation of the program would have to be made in order for that third party to run it.

Files and copyright issues

The ready availability of **Internet** access and of **multi-media input/output devices** such as **digital cameras** and **scanners** raises important issues relating to the copyright status of files, such as music files, images and so on. Basically, any **image**, **text file**, **music file** or **video file**, unless created by, written by, composed or filmed by the user is protected by internationally recognised copyright legislation. <u>This means that no copy, either in paper form or digital format, of any type of material, may be created without the permission of the owner of the copyright.</u> The copyright owner is deemed to be the author/creator of the original item, or, in the case of an organisation, the employer of the author/creator.

Driving Lesson 72 - Continued

The effect of this legislation is that **any** text or picture **scanned** into a PC and saved; any **image**, **text file**, **music** or **video file** downloaded from the Internet and saved to disk is **illegal**, unless specifically identified by its owner as being **copyright-free**. This situation also applies to any digital material saved on **removable media** such as **memory sticks** and **CD/DVD**s. This material must be considered to be copyright protected unless distributed by its owner, or specifically identified as being **copyright-free**. Effectively, therefore, it should not be **used or distributed**!

Software Licenses

As discussed earlier, a typical piece of software is sold with a **single user licence**, allowing only one installation of the software to be carried out. In order to cater for the situation within an organisation where a software application is used by all employees, multi-user **site licences** can be purchased. Any licence would have to cover the likely maximum number of users. The penalties for infringement of software copyright laws can be very severe indeed!

When a piece of software is installed on a computer, there is usually a point in the installation process where the user has to enter their own name and/or their company name. There is another stage when the user has to signify (usually by ticking a check box) that they have read and accepted the **End User Agreement**. This is the document mentioned earlier, which details exactly what the user is permitted to do with the software. The **End User Agreement** is usually displayed in a scrolling dialog box at the same stage as the indication of acceptance by the user. Without this acceptance, installation will not proceed.

Product ID

Once a legitimate software installation has been completed, the details you have entered are locked to that application. Each individual example of the program has its own **registration number** known as the **Product ID**. It is possible to view this information to check that this version of the software is licensed to a particular person. The information can usually be displayed by clicking on **Help** on the **Menu Bar** and selecting **About**.

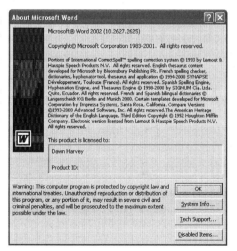

Driving Lesson 72 - Continued

Shareware is a type of software that can be obtained on the equivalent of a sale-or-return basis. The software is obtained and distributed free of charge and installed for a pre-determined trial period, typically 30 days. At the end of this evaluation period, the software is programmed either to cease operating, or to flash up reminders, unless a payment is made to the author/software house.

Another type of shareware is software that is available free of initial fee, but is not the fully functioning version of the program. The watered down version allows the potential of the package to be evaluated, but the operator must then pay to receive the full version, together with registration and technical support as an official user. The main advantage of shareware is its cost. Relative to major commercial packages, useful software can be acquired extremely cheaply, often in the £10-£30 price range.

Freeware is, as the term implies, available completely free of any purchase or licensing fee. It is provided by programmers, who write software for their own interest and are then prepared to make the fruits of their labours available to others. Shareware can originate from a similar source, but the author presumably has decided to recoup some reward for his/her efforts.

Open Source software provides the source code for the software under a licence, allowing users to change and improve the software; they can then redistribute it.

 Manoeuvres

1. What does the purchase of a **single-user licence** allow a software user to do?

2. Discuss some pros and cons of using **shareware/freeware**.

Driving Lesson 73 - The Data Protection Act

◨ Park and Read

The Data Protection Act (1998) regulates the use of personal data by all businesses. It aims to promote high standards in the handling of personal information, and so to protect the individual's right to privacy. This act defines personal data as any data that can be used to identify a living individual, including names, addresses, personalised e-mail addresses and video images of such individuals, e.g. medical records, employee records.

Data Controller

Under the Data Protection Act (1998), a person who determines the purposes for which and the manner in which any personal data is to be processed, is the **data controller**. In a business that is not run by a sole trader, or that is not a partnership, the business itself is defined as the data controller.

The law requires data controllers to give their details to the Information Commissioner's Office for inclusion in a public register, unless their data processing is exempt. This is so that people can find out who is processing personal data about them and why they are doing so.

The Act sets out eight rules that data controllers must follow for protecting personal data; these are known as the eight principles. Personal data must be:

♦ Obtained and processed fairly and lawfully.

♦ Processed only for one or more specified and lawful purposes.

♦ Adequate, relevant and not excessive for those purposes.

♦ Accurate and kept up to date.

♦ Kept for no longer than is necessary for the purposes for which it is being processed.

♦ Processed in line with the rights of the individual.

♦ Secure and protected against loss, damage and inappropriate processing.

♦ Not transferred to countries outside the European Economic Area unless there is adequate protection for the information.

Driving Lesson 73 - Continued

If a business does not comply with the principles, the Information Commissioner can take enforcement action against the data controller, whether it is an individual or a business.

Data Subject

This is the individual who has data kept about them. The data subject has the right:

- ♦ to be informed when information is being held

- ♦ to be told the purpose for which it is held

- ♦ to know to whom the data will be disclosed

- ♦ to refuse to allow their details to be used for direct marketing.

Manoeuvres

1.   What type of information is covered by the **Data Protection Act**?

2.   Describe the **Data Protection Principles**.

Driving Lesson 74 - Revision

This Driving Lesson covers the features introduced in this section. Try not to refer to the preceding Driving Lessons while completing it.

1. What does **backing store** mean and why is it important?

2. How can **unauthorised access** to computer file systems be prevented?

3. What can happen to **data and files** in the event of a power cut?

4. What is the difference between a **User ID** and a **Password**?

5. What do you understand by the term **access rights**?

6. Detail four issues that an effective **Information Security Policy** should set out.

7. How can a **computer virus** enter a system?

8. Name three different types of **virus**.

9. Explain the difference between a **virus** and a **bug**.

10. Why is it important to update **anti-virus** software on a regular basis?

11. What do you understand by the term **software copyright**?

12. How do **shareware** and **freeware** differ from mainstream software?

13. Why may it be illegal to distribute images which have been downloaded from an unknown source on removable media?

14. Give an overview of the implications of the **Data Protection Act** for computer users.

If you experienced any difficulty completing the Revision, refer back to the Driving Lessons in this section. Then redo the Revision. Once you are confident with the features, complete the Record of Achievement Matrix referring to the section at the end of the guide.

Answers

Please note: these are example answers only.

Driving Lesson 31

Step 10 The **Modified** date is shown as 17 February 1993.

Step 11 **Cam.docx**.

Driving Lesson 32

Step 1 **Marketing**, a *PowerPoint* presentation.

Step 3

Name	In Folder
Advert.docx	C:\Documents and Settings\SarahTerry\My Documents\CIA DATA FILES...
Banking.docx	C:\Documents and Settings\SarahTerry\My Documents\CIA DATA FILES...
Cam.docx	C:\Documents and Settings\SarahTerry\My Documents\CIA DATA FILES...
CIA Training Ltd - Overview.docx	C:\Documents and Settings\SarahTerry\My Documents\CIA DATA FILES...
Clothing.docx	C:\Documents and Settings\SarahTerry\My Documents\CIA DATA FILES...
Contents.docx	C:\Documents and Settings\SarahTerry\My Documents\CIA DATA FILES...

Step 6 12 files

Step 7 13 files.

Driving Lesson 37

Step 2 This will vary between computers but commonly, **A4**.

Step 3 Right click the selected printer icon in the **Printers and Faxes** window and select the **Set as Default Printer** option.

Step 7 This will vary between computers.

Step 9 You might need to align print cartridges after installing or replacing a cartridge, if printed characters are not properly formed, if the margins are misaligned or if straight lines look wavy.

Driving Lesson 52

Step 4 **Revision.zip** is 340 KB and the **Managing Files** folder is 745KB.

Driving Lesson 56

Step 1   False. They can totally destroy data.

Step 2   False. Any computer can be infected.

Step 3   True.

Step 4   True.

Step 5   True.

Step 6   False. They can lie dormant.

Step 7   False. Many applications will remove viruses.

Step 8   True.

Step 9   False. It needs to be updated on a regular basis.

Step 10   True.

Step 11   Possible costs involved in having a virus in the system include:

Before detection, the virus could cause poor computer performance, system crashes, etc.

Once detected, computers will be out of action until the virus is dealt with.

External consultants employed to remove virus.

Re-keying any lost data.

Fraudulent transactions due to security breaches.

Apologising to any customers, contacts, etc. who may have been inadvertently infected with the virus before it was detected.

Driving Lesson 63

Step 10   The left slider in the **Volume Control** dialog box follows the movement of the single volume slider.

Driving Lesson 67

Step 1   Routine maintenance should be performed to keep your computer healthy and running at peak performance.

Step 2   Use the **Disk Cleanup** tool or delete the files yourself on a regular basis.

Step 3   Clean an optical mouse by simply wiping thoroughly with a paper towel dampened with a mild cleaning agent.

Step 4   Sources of help: help menus, manufacturers' manuals, IT admin, technicians, colleagues, help lines.

Driving Lesson 68

Step 1   You would make sure your workplace was safe by checking for: trailing or insecure power leads or cables, worn or frayed power leads, overloaded power points.

Step 2   An employee is responsible for making proper use of provisions and going about their job in a responsible manner.

Step 3   To protect the environment you could recycle waste paper, ink and toner cartridges, use monitors with low power options and PCs with standby mode. You could also save documents rather than print out hard copies.

Driving Lesson 69

Step 1   **HASAW** is Health and Safety at Work.

Step 2   A good working environment would be well lit and ventilated, have glare free VDUs, adjustable chairs and mouse mats provided. There would be provision for breaks from the computer.

Step 3   **RSI** is repetitive strain injury.

Step 4   Check for: trailing or insecure power leads or cables, worn or frayed power leads, overloaded power points. Make sure your chair is at the correct angle for your back and your feet touch the floor, that your monitor screen is free from glare and you have regular breaks.

Step 5   Some common injuries: back ache due to poor posture, RSI, eye strain and trips or falls.

Step 6   **Ergonomics** means the relationship between workers and their environment.

Step 7   To save paper you can recycle it and save files to disk rather than print them.

Driving Lesson 70

Step 1   You should regularly save to permanent storage in case the computer crashes, there is a power failure, or there is some physical, permanent damage to the computer.

Step 2   At least one set of backing store media should be kept off site because of the risk of fire, theft or flood.

Step 3   Possible levels of password protection for networked files: a password to access the PC, a user ID to access the network, a password to access the directory or network server, a password to access the file, a password to amend the file content.

Driving Lesson 72

Step 1   A single user licence allows the software to be installed only once.

Step 2   Advantages of shareware/freeware: either cheaper than major commercial packages or totally free. Disadvantages: shareware is either a not fully functioning version of the software, or will shut down after a trial period unless a fee is paid.

Driving Lesson 73

Step 1   Personal information, e.g. names, addresses, financial information, etc. is covered by the Data Protection Act.

Step 2   The Data Protection Principles are conventions that must be followed by all organisations keeping information.

Driving Lesson 74

Step 1   Backing store is storage containing backed up material and is important because it may be needed due to computer failure, damage, etc.

Step 2   Unauthorised access to files can be prevented by applying passwords to every level of access.

Step 3   In the event of a power cut any changes made to data and files since they were last saved may be lost.

Step 4   A user ID lets the system know that the user is entitled to access the network and also which level of access is allowed. A password is a user's personal entry code to a computer, software or files.

Step 5   Access rights are the different levels of access allowed by different user IDs.

Step 6   Any four of the following: details of a user ID/password; the personnel responsible for each level of security; anti-virus measures specified by the security policy; penalties for breaching security policy; procedures for reporting security incidents; procedures for educating staff about their responsibilities relating to information security.

Step 7   A virus can enter a system through an e-mail attachment, floppy disk, CD or DVD, or the Internet.

Step 8   Any three of the following: time bomb/logic bomb, macro virus, worm, Trojan Horse.

Step 9   A virus is a malicious piece of programming intended to cause harm, but a bug is an error or fault in a piece of software code.

Step 10 Anti-virus software should be regularly updated because new viruses appear every day.

Step 11 Software copyright gives authors and developers of software the same legal protection as authors of published, written and musical works.

Step 12 Shareware and freeware are cheaper than mainstream software (or free). Shareware often has a free trial period or a trial of a cut down version of the program, before the fee is payable.

Step 13 This material must be considered copyright protected and it is therefore illegal to distribute it.

Step 14 For data holders, the Data Protection Act means they must ensure the data is secure and disclosed only for legitimate purposes. They must only hold relevant material and nothing more. The data must be accurate and up to date and not held when it is no longer needed. The information must also be accessible to the individual concerned.

Glossary

Application	A stand-alone piece of software which can be used for a specific purpose.
Archive	A file containing one or more compressed files.
Autorun	A program on a CD, DVD or floppy disk which starts running as soon as the disk is loaded.
Backing up	Making copies of all important files
Compact Disk Drive	A device used to read and write to and from Compact Disks.
Compact Disk	Also known as CD's, these contain hundreds of megabytes of information.
Compress	Use special software to save a file or group of files so that they take up much less space.
Computer Virus	A malicious piece of code which can cause damage to computerised systems.
Control Panel	An area on the computer from which the user can perform advanced administrative tasks.
Desktop	The first display screen of *Windows* from which all other applications are run.
Drivers	Software which enables an application to use a specific hardware device, e.g. printer.
Firewall	A filter to control traffic from your PC to the Internet and vice versa.
Floppy Disk Drive	A device used to hold, add and remove data from 3.5inch floppy disks.
Floppy Disk	A small capacity external storage device.
Folder	A method of grouping together files (and other folders).
Formatting (text)	Changing the appearance of text. Any text from a single word to a whole document can be formatted.
Hard Drive	Also known as HDD, the Hard Drive is a large storage medium on which files can be saved.
Hardware	Any physical part of a computer system.
Icon	A small visual representation of an application.
Keyboard	An input device used to enter text into a computer.
Monitor	A visual display unit used to show the user information about what the computer is doing.

Mouse	An input device which is used to control the cursor on the **Desktop** area of the computer screen.
Multimedia	An application or function that involves many techniques such as text, sound and video.
Multiple Selection	Selecting several files and/or folders from a display so that an action can be applied to all of them.
Notepad	A basic text editing application supplied with *Windows*.
Power Switch	A switch usually found on the front of the system unit which supplies power to the computer.
Print Preview	Allows a user to see on screen how a document will look when printed.
Print Queue	A list of print requests waiting to be processed by a printer.
Read-only	A property given to a file or folder which means that it cannot be amended.
Recycle Bin	An area of storage where deleted files are held temporarily before being deleted completely.
Shortcut	An icon (usually found on the **Desktop** area) which opens an application stored elsewhere.
Subfolder	A folder that is contained within another folder.
Taskbar	By default, a blue bar running the length of the **Desktop**, at the bottom of the screen. Shows which tasks the computer is performing.
Wizard	A program that guides a user through a complex task by asking a series of questions.
Zipping	Another name for compressing a file.

Index

Record of Achievement Matrix

This Matrix is to be used to measure your progress while working through the guide. This is a learning reinforcement process, you judge when you are competent.

Tick boxes are provided for each feature. 1 is for no knowledge, 2 some knowledge and 3 is for competent. A section is only complete when column 3 is completed for all parts of the section.

For details on sitting ECDL Examinations in your country please contact the local ECDL Licensee or visit the European Computer Driving Licence Foundation Limited web site at http://www.ecdl.org.

Tick the Relevant Boxes **1**: No Knowledge   **2**: Some Knowledge   **3**: Competent

Section	No.	Driving Lesson	1	2	3
1 Getting Started	1	Preparation			
	2	Starting the Computer			
	3	The Windows Desktop			
	4	Arranging Icons			
	5	The Taskbar			
	6	The Start Menu			
	7	Opening Windows			
	8	Sizing and Moving Windows			
	9	Scroll Bars			
	10	Close a Window			
	11	System Properties			
	12	Using Help			
	13	Shut Down and Restart			
2 Managing Files	15	File Storage			
	16	Folders and Files			
	17	Folder View			
	18	File Types			
	19	Sorting File Displays			
	20	Creating New Folders			
	21	Copying Files and Folders			
	22	Moving Files and Folders			
	23	Selecting Multiple Files			
	24	Viewing Object Properties			
	25	Renaming Files and Folders			
	26	Deleting Files and Folders			
	27	The Recycle Bin			
	28	Copy a Floppy Disk			
	29	Searching for Files/Folders			
	30	Advanced Searching			

Tick the Relevant Boxes **1**: No Knowledge   **2**: Some Knowledge   **3**: Competent

Section	No.	Driving Lesson	1	2	3
3 Print Management	33	Printers			
	34	Add a New Printer			
	35	Print Jobs			
	36	Printer Maintenance			
4 Running Applications	38	Run an Application			
	39	Entering and Formatting Text			
	40	Saving Text			
	41	Print a Document			
	42	Using Print Screen			
	43	Switch Between Applications			
	44	Closing an Application			
	45	Install/Uninstall an Application			
	46	Create Desktop Icons			
	47	Use Desktop Icons			
5 Using Compress	49	File Compression			
	50	Compress Files			
	51	Uncompress Files			
6 Virus Control	53	Computer Viruses			
	54	Anti-Virus Protection			
	55	Anti-Virus Protection Applications			
7 The Control Panel	57	Control Panel			
	58	Date/Time			
	59	Display Options			
	60	Screen Saver			
	61	Settings and Effects			
	62	Sound			

Tick the Relevant Boxes **1**: No Knowledge   **2**: Some Knowledge   **3**: Competent

Section	No.	Driving Lesson	1	2	3
8 Systems Maintenance	64	Maintaining Systems			
	65	Cleaning Hardware			
	66	Dealing with Problems			
9 Health & Safety Environment	68	Health and Safety			
10 Security	70	Security Issues			
	71	Safe and Proper Practice			
	72	Copyright			
	73	The Data Protection Act			